PSALMS TO CALM THE MOM

PSALMS TO CALM THE MOM

BOYS TO MEN: TRANSITION IS MESSY

CHARLI DELL

CONTENTS

FORWARD

Psalms To Calm the Mom-Boys to Men, The Transition is Messy

It has been an amazing journey of growing, stretching and learning, as my husband and I have raised five children. If there is one thing I would want you to get out of this book it is this. Never stop. Never stop believing, never stop hoping and never stop praying. God can make a way where there seems to be no way. I have learned there is no formula. Yes, there are tips and strategies and helpful hints, but none of them work on every child. No matter how many children you come in contact with or how many children you "train up in the way of the Lord" the next one will surprise you. In this way God keeps us coming back for His daily bread. There is a lot of wisdom that David wrote down for us in the Psalms, but the bottom line is this: <u>"Yet will I trust thee."</u>

Meet my Children: Please note that the names and places and sometimes facts have been changed to protect the guilty. I have no intention of hanging out dirty laundry about my children. On the other hand I would like the freedom to be real, honest and if necessary share the dirty truth about my wicked imagination and how God's mercy pulled me out of that pit, time and time again.

Tony is 19 as I write this, he is in college. He comes home for special occasions and to raid the place for food which I readily supply because, after all, I don't want my baby boy to starve.

Jason is 20. He and I are so much alike that he could have been my twin if he'd been born earlier. We have gone round and round because of our similar personalities. But he too is out of the house on his own...mostly. I believe he has amazing talent in certain areas but, for now, he has chosen to work in the construction business.

My daughter, Rachel, 22, is also in college. She also comes home now and then to raid the fridge of leftovers and spend some quality time, (sleeping in, watching movies) with her parents, as well as seek some peace from all the hustle and bustle of city life.

My two older daughters Leah and Ruth are married and live several hours away. They are married to my two amazing son-in-loves, Richard and John, whom I consider two more sons gained. They have busy lives but we find time to get together four or five times a year. Yes I intend to write my next book about the girls, no one goes untouched.

I have been married for more than thirty years to my amazing husband, Dave. (D) It took me quite a while to realize that he was amazing and to appreciate his better qualities, but that is for another book!

I hope you will enjoy this 31 day journey through the Psalms. Some of it may be eye opening, or toe stomping. The best thing to do is own it, confess it and move forward with God, ever growing, learning, changing and being transformed into His image. It is only by His grace and mercy that any of us can do that. This devotional will be focusing on my boys. They are the youngest in the family and the most recent graduates into adult life. Much of this book will talk about their difficult transition into the adult world and my naivety, believing I could save them from God's refining fire. Keep in mind that these are not in the order they happened but often in order of the relevant Psalm.

May the Lord bless you on this journey, but also change you. Father, I offer up this small token of truth, a piece of a huge educational pie. Maybe I can save others from the anger and hurt that comes from trying to fix a person from the outside in, instead of letting you handle it from the inside out. You are our God and we will ever praise you. Teach us to also glorify you in all we do and say, especially towards our children. May your will be done every hour of the day and the words of our mouths and the meditation of our hearts be acceptable to you. In your name, by your power, Amen

I suggest you keep a journal handy so you can personalize the prayers in this 31 day devotional.

Deuteronomy 11:19 And ye shall teach them your children, speaking of them when thou sittest in thine house, and when thou walkest by the way, when thou liest down, and when thou risest up. Write a prayer for yourself and your children. What does teaching your children to Love the Lord your God look like to you? What scriptures and truths are important in your walk with the Lord that you want to share with them?

THE PERFECT MOM

Psalm 1:1-6 Blessed is the man that walketh not in the counsel of the ungodly, nor standeth in the way of sinners, nor sitteth in the seat of the scornful. But his delight is in the law of the LORD; and in his law doth he meditate day and night. And he shall be like a tree planted by the rivers of water, that bringeth forth his fruit in his season; his leaf also shall not wither; and whatsoever he doeth shall prosper. The ungodly are not so: but are like the chaff which the wind driveth away. Therefore the ungodly shall not stand in the judgment, nor sinners in the congregation of the righteous. For the LORD knoweth the way of the righteous: but the way of the ungodly shall perish.

Expectations; they can be killers of hope. Maybe your hopes weren't as high as mine. I pictured a doctor for my first born, number two, a missionary, then a concert pianist, another Billy Graham and lastly, Vice President of the United States for the youngest. Ok, I'll admit my expectations were a little high. I'll even admit I set myself and my kids up for failure. I honestly didn't even realize I was doing it until things didn't pan out quite the way I thought they should. This may come as a surprise to you but my kids...get this... are "normal". Not only that but every single one of them are sinners. I KNOW! You are shocked, aren't you? Another expectation was that my kids would "arrive" at full wisdom and knowledge by the time they reached the age of 18. How I could have thought that when I am over 50 and STILL haven't arrived is beyond me. Of course, now that the fog has lifted I know that none of us will arrive until we go to our heavenly home!

On a different note, we have an enemy that goes around like a roaring lion that loves nothing better than to set us up for a fall. High, unrealistic expectations of ourselves and our children can wreak havoc. My goal was to be the perfect parent. When Psalm 1 talks about a tree that's planted by living waters it's talking about being constantly plugged into God. Who we are as a mom, who God created us to be, can be so much better when we stay connected to God. How do we do that? Just like you would a friend, read his letters daily, and talk to him all the time, about everything. "Pray without ceasing." Tell him thank-you for everything from being able to breathe to having enough food on the table. And ask for help. My favorite prayer is asking for wisdom. **James 1:5 If any of you lack wisdom, let him ask of God, that giveth to all men liberally, and upbraideth not; and it shall be given him.** He will give it, but we have to humble ourselves enough to ask! I love his gifts of grace and mercy because he is constantly giving us second, third and fourth chances.

Challenge: There is no guarantee that our children will turn out "right" but there is a guarantee that **"he who has begun a good work in them will perform it until the day" Php. 1:6**, all the way up until Jesus comes back. Trust him, stay in his word and research what Proverbs 22:6 <u>really means</u>. **"Train up a child in the way he should go: and when he is old, he will not depart from it."** Recognize that none of us are "perfect" trainers, no matter how bad we want to be, and therefore there are no guarantees. So don't do it for the payoff of perfect kids; do it as unto the Lord.

Prayer: Lord, please bless my children that they will not walk in the counsel of the ungodly, nor stand in the way of sinners, nor sit in the seat of the mouthy. Let their delight be in obeying you and knowing your word day and night. Help them to be like a tree planted by the rivers of water, which bring forth it's fruit at the right time, healthy and full of hope, so that all they do will be successful. Please Lord protect them from becoming ungodly, don't let them be like the chaff which the wind drives away. Help them to be righteous and stand up for what is right. You know LORD the way of the righteous, please teach it to my children.

DAY 2

MOM POWER

Psalms 2 Psalms 2:1-12 Why do the heathen rage, and the people imagine a vain thing? The kings of the earth set themselves, and the rulers take counsel together, against the LORD, and against his anointed, saying, Let us break their bands asunder, and cast away their cords from us. He that sitteth in the heavens shall laugh: the Lord shall have them in derision. Then shall he speak unto them in his wrath, and vex them in his sore displeasure. Yet have I set my king upon my holy hill of Zion. I will declare the decree: the LORD hath said unto me, Thou art my Son; this day have I begotten thee. Ask of me, and I shall give thee the heathen for thine inheritance, and the uttermost parts of the earth for thy possession. Thou shalt break them with a rod of iron; thou shalt dash them in pieces like a potter's vessel. Be wise now therefore, O ye kings: be instructed, ye judges of the earth. Serve the LORD with fear, and rejoice with trembling. Kiss the Son, lest he be angry, and ye perish from the way, when his wrath is kindled but a little. <u>Blessed are all they that put their trust in him.</u>

Many times I have sat back and evaluated my place in the home. At the drop of five words I can turn the attitude of the whole household upside down. **"To whom much is given, much is required"**. Luke

12:48 I used to resent all that power. My husband D doesn't have that much power. There were times when I felt like I was trudging up the mountain holding a rope over my shoulder, with my children lined up behind me holding the rope. My husband is bringing up the rear. I would stop, look over my shoulder and say, "HEY, you need to get up here and pull for a little while, I'm tired!" He would come up to the front, tell all the kids to let go and take them out for a coke or something. Because of my own complaining, I set myself up to be the disciplinarian. I, after all, had read all the books and knew how to do it right! "Pride cometh before a fall". D was not willing to be reprimanded or taught by me, so being the gentleman he is he stepped back and let me handle it....until the boys got too old and needed their dad. Don't get me wrong, I do believe that there is a right way and a wrong way to discipline, but if you are constantly complaining or trying to teach the "by the book" method to your husband, expect him to bow out. In Ephesians 5 the husband is often interchanged with Christ or Lord. **Ephesians 5:23-25 For the husband is the head of the wife, even as Christ is the head of the church: and he is the saviour of the body. Therefore as the church is subject unto Christ, so let the wives be to their own husbands in every thing. Husbands, love your wives, even as Christ also loved the church, and gave himself for it;** These words are hard for a strong, controlling woman like myself to hear. Why would God make me this way if he were not going to make me a man? D, on the other hand, is laid back and calm! It took me a long time to figure it out but I finally realized it's for protection. I also realized D's job is a lot more difficult than mine; he has to lay down his life for me. **Ephesians 5:25** I just have to ask permission every once in a while... which is a good thing considering the stability of my hormones and the rationale of my mind during certain times of the month. Even so, many times, because of D's job, the dealings with teenage problems would fall to me.

Challenge: Become a united front with your husband and a threefold cord with Jesus. **Ecclesiastes 4:12** If you are a single parent become a united front with Jesus, constantly asking for wisdom and listening for answers.

Prayer: Abba, Father, Please control my thoughts. Don't let my imaginations run away with me. Help me to keep my eyes on you and not jump to the worst conclusion possible at a moment's notice. Keep my mind stayed on you, not on every conceivable bad thing that can happen to my children. Don't let me try to step into your place of power to "fix" my children from the outside in. I know that is fruitless, because I've tried it so many times. I don't want to walk on my own. I want your power; it's so much greater than my vain imaginations! I want to honor you. I am your child. Yet you have given me much and even in my own home I have "much power". Help me to be wise with what you have given me. Give me the grace to serve you with fear and rejoice in you with trembling. I will honor you, and I will put my trust in you through the power of your Holy Spirit. Amen.

NO SUCH THING

Psalm 3:1-8 LORD, how are they increased that trouble me! many are they that rise up against me. Many there be which say of my soul, There is no help for him in God. Selah. But thou, O LORD, art a shield for me; my glory, and the lifter up of mine head. I cried unto the LORD with my voice, and he heard me out of his holy hill. Selah. I laid me down and slept; I awaked; for the LORD sustained me. I will not be afraid of ten thousands of people, that have set themselves against me round about. Arise, O LORD; save me, O my God: for thou hast smitten all mine enemies upon the cheek bone; thou hast broken the teeth of the ungodly. Salvation belongeth unto the LORD: thy blessing is upon thy people. Selah.

Never think that King David didn't have his own problems with kids! Fleeing from your own son has to be incredibly humbling. And the, "Where did I go wrong" questions, I'm sure, poured over him. The first time I realized that my children had a will of their own and they were not going to take my advice and do things the easy way, I was stunned. We were at church every time the doors were open. Note: Going to church doesn't make you spiritual and righteous. Granted it helps your children come to Christ if they can hear the gospel over and over again, but they can learn many other things at church too, from other sinners. Gasp! I know, right? We read scriptures almost every day. Note: Reading scriptures and knowing the word of God may give your kids wisdom, and it is powerful; but it does not guarantee that they will not be tempted and led astray. Now you're thinking, "Well, what is the secret?" Remember my disclaimer, <u>there is no formula</u>. Ok, that's not entirely true: Do what God calls you to do and leave the rest up to him.

Challenge: Listen; Half the time we feel like we are guessing about what God is calling us to do- that scripture in John, **"My sheep hear my voice, and I know them, and they follow me:" John 10:27** I am his sheep, but I STILL have trouble hearing what he's saying among the other thousands of voices in my head. Ok, maybe I'm stubborn, and I might've even thought I knew better then God at times; but I'm past that now. Let me tell you what I <u>do</u> know without a doubt. 1. He loves me, and he loves you. 2. First and foremost he calls us to love him and to love others; because love is powerful, in fact it is "the greatest of these". If you don't know what love looks like read 1 Corinthians 13. 3. Ask for wisdom. I cannot count the times that I have run to God and said, "HEEELLLP!! I don't know what to do!" And the answer came to me.

Prayer: Sometimes, Lord, I feel like I am one against the world. People with perfect children (ok, in reality I know there is no such thing) feel sorry for me and truly believe "There is no help for her in God." But you, O LORD, are a shield for me; my glory and the lifter of my head, when I just want to crawl into a hole. I called on you for help and wisdom and you heard me. Because of your grace and peace I can actually sleep in the midst of turmoil. Help me to stay in today, because when I travel into the future I am terrified.

But you have helped me recognize Satan's tactics and saved me from worry and strife. "When I am afraid I will trust in you." You are my salvation, not perfect children, not a perfect life, but you alone. Thank-you for your thousands of blessings upon me and my family. Amen

DAY 4

GRACE AND MERCY

Psalm 4:1-Hear me when I call, O God of my righteousness: thou hast enlarged me when I was in distress; have mercy upon me, and hear my prayer. O ye sons of men, how long will ye turn my glory into shame? how long will ye love vanity, and seek after leasing? Selah. But know that the LORD hath set apart him that is godly for himself: the LORD will hear when I call unto him. Stand in awe, and sin not: commune with your own heart upon your bed, and be still. Selah. Offer the sacrifices of righteousness, and put your trust in the LORD. There be many that say, Who will shew us any good? LORD, lift thou up the light of thy countenance upon us. Thou hast put gladness in my heart, more than in the time that their corn and their wine increased. I will both lay me down in peace, and sleep: for thou, LORD, only makest me dwell in safety.

It was not his first love but he was naïve. I warned him, but he didn't have the knowledge to keep his distance. He trusted in his own strength and was sucked in. **"And beheld among the simple ones, I discerned among the youths, a young man void of understanding, passing through the street near her corner; and he went the way to her house..."Pr. 7:7,8** She was beautiful, and fun to be around, but I suspected from the beginning that nothing good could come from it. They were so young. But something good did come, it brought him to his knees. Tony was best friends with her brother. There was one key element missing in the whole relationship. Trust. He knew it, but he could not bring himself to walk away. Like the young man in Proverbs he was led to the slaughter. He was a knight in shining armor. He rescued her over and over again. Through his grace and mercy towards her he learned of the grace of God towards him.

As a mom, it is difficult to watch your son's heart being ripped out over and over again. It was the closest thing to witchcraft I had seen in a long time. It was terrifying to see my son, who normally is full of wisdom, be reeled in like a fish on a hook. Not just one time, but over and over again. **"She is loud and stubborn; her feet abide not in her house:"** She had joy, she reminded me of me when I was her age. It took months before the ties were finally broken for good, all the ties. No more best friend, no more relationships with the parents, no more going back, no more rescuing. The aftermath was devastating but God is still on the throne and Tony is healing.

Challenge: Work on trust factors and relationships with your kids. Listen to what they are saying and listen to what they are not saying. Start when they are young. Keep their confidence. They will need you when they become teenagers. They will need a friend they can trust as well as a parent they can seek advice from and one that will love them unconditionally. The challenge is knowing when to speak and knowing when to be quiet. Pray for the future spouse of your children and pray for them to have the wisdom to "guard their hearts". (Pr. 4:23)

For God hath not given us the spirit of fear; but of power, and of love, and of a sound mind. 2 Timothy 1:7

Prayer: Hear my children when they call, O God of their righteousness: You have helped them in the past when they were in distress, please have mercy upon them and hear my prayer. They have turned your glory into shame and love worthless things and seek after lies. But they know you, and you have begun a good work in them. You will protect them from their own foolishness because you love them. By the blood of Jesus Christ they are righteous, they have accepted you. Help them to stand in awe and not sin. Give them the grace to trust you. Shine your light on them. You have put gladness in my heart. I will sleep in peace and trust you because you only can make them dwell in safety. Please, Lord, bring a godly women in the lives of my sons who will draw them to you, not carry them away. Give them the ability to find a good wife, it is the second most important decision they will ever make. In Jesus name, by your grace, Amen

DAY 5

GOD IS GREATER

Psalm 5:1-12 Give ear to my words, O LORD, consider my meditation. Hearken unto the voice of my cry, my King, and my God: for unto thee will I pray. My voice shalt thou hear in the morning, O LORD; in the morning will I direct my prayer unto thee, and will look up. For thou art not a God that hath pleasure in wickedness: neither shall evil dwell with thee. The foolish shall not stand in thy sight: thou hatest all workers of iniquity. Thou shalt destroy them that speak leasing: the LORD will abhor the bloody and deceitful man. But as for me, I will come into thy house in the multitude of thy mercy: and in thy fear will I worship toward thy holy temple. Lead me, O LORD, in thy righteousness because of mine enemies; make thy way straight before my face. For there is no faithfulness in their mouth; their inward part is very wickedness; their throat is an open sepulchre; they flatter with their tongue. Destroy thou them, O God; let them fall by their own counsels; cast them out in the multitude of their transgressions; for they have rebelled against thee. But let all those that put their trust in thee rejoice: let them ever shout for joy, because thou defendest them: let them also that love thy name be joyful in thee. For thou, LORD, wilt bless the righteous; with favour wilt thou compass him as with a shield.

Many times as I pray for my children I look in the mirror and think, I am no farther along than they are! Sometimes I seem to rise and fall with the tide. My faith wavers like the waves of the ocean. **The LORD redeemeth the soul of his servants: and none of them that trust in him shall be desolate. Psalm 34:22** Trust is a pretty big factor in God's eyes; **"Without faith it is impossible to please him". Heb 11:6** So what does faith look like? For me it is saying over and over again three words, reminding myself God can do anything. Jason is telling lies and spreading them around. Sometimes I'm not sure, does he truly believe what he is saying? Perhaps I'm being overly judgmental. No, we've actually had proof and still he tried to cover it up with more lies. Is he a worker of iniquity? Here are the three words, "<u>God is greater</u>". Look at all the negative words that King David speaks in Psalm 5. Evil, wickedness, foolish, workers of iniquity [trouble], speak leasing [lies]. All of these words can be said of King David! He killed Bathsheba's husband to cover up his sin of adultery! **2 Sam 11:15** And yet David was **"the apple of God's eye".Ps 17:8** How does that even work? The difference is David humbled himself and had a **"broken and contrite [regretful] heart" .Ps 51:17** It wasn't because David was perfect. God showed mercy to David, and he can do the same for us and our children because God is greater than anything we can do or say.

Challenge: Trust God. Stop worrying. Make up your mind to start listening to God's truth instead of Satan's lies. Speak it out loud. <u>God is greater</u>. God, I know you can change the heart from the inside out. I know you created him. You know him. You know what it will take to change his heart.

Don't tell your kids what they already know; "You are a sinner and you keep messing up." Tell them what they don't know. "God has a plan for your life. He is working on you every second of the day, and whether you feel it or not, he is right beside you everywhere you go. He will not leave you because he loves you. He will not give up on you, and no matter how deep you go down into that pit of lies, God will go deeper still to pull you out." **Ps 139:7** God changed Jacob the deceiver into Israel a prince. **Gen. 32:28** Truth: God is greater.

Prayer: Thank you God that you hear my voice, even when I don't feel sincere, even when I feel selfish and whiney and weak. **"My grace is sufficient for thee: for my strength is made perfect in weakness. Most gladly therefore will I rather glory in my infirmities, that the power of Christ may rest upon me." 2 Cor 12:9** In the night I pray for my children, Lord please don't let them be workers of iniquity, stop them in their tracks. Please suck the foolishness and lies out of their minds and fill them with wisdom so they can put their trust in you and find joy. Give them the grace to speak the truth. Help us to love your name and trust your word. Thank-you that we are righteous because of the blood of Jesus Christ. Protect us with your shield of righteousness. We are all weak and go astray and lose our way. Lead us back to the truth. We are nothing without you, our works are filthy rags, we cannot even breathe without your mercy. Infuse us with the power of your Holy Spirit so that we can be "meet for the master's use". **2 Tim. 2:21** Amen

DAY 6

TAKE TIME TO TALK

Psalms 6 O LORD, rebuke me not in thine anger, neither chasten me in thy hot displeasure. Have mercy upon me, O LORD; for I am weak: O LORD, heal me; for my bones are vexed. My soul is also sore vexed: but thou, O LORD, how long? Return, O LORD, deliver my soul: oh save me for thy mercies' sake. For in death there is no remembrance of thee: in the grave who shall give thee thanks? I am weary with my groaning; all the night make I my bed to swim; I water my couch with my tears. Mine eye is consumed because of grief; it waxeth old because of all mine enemies. Depart from me, all ye workers of iniquity; for the LORD hath heard the voice of my weeping. The LORD hath heard my supplication; the LORD will receive my prayer. Let all mine enemies be ashamed and sore vexed: let them return and be ashamed suddenly.

Much of the time teenagers won't talk until after 10 or 11 at night. Wait, it's worth the sleep loss. Make the sacrifice and stay up and listen. I have told my kids that they can tell me anything. "I may freak out the first five minutes," I said, "just let me vent, then I will settle down and we can find a solution to this problem together." Sometimes we all think we are in this alone, we have no one to talk to, no one to go to. Even King David felt like the Lord had left him.

"Have mercy upon me, O LORD; for I am weak: O LORD, heal me; for my bones are vexed. My soul is also sore vexed: but thou, O LORD, how long? Return, O LORD, deliver my soul: oh save me for thy mercies' sake. For in death there is no remembrance of thee: in the grave who shall give thee thanks?" Our enemies are just as real now as they were to David. **1 Peter 5:8 Be sober, be vigilant; because your adversary the devil, as a roaring lion, walketh about, seeking whom he may devour:** I'm not asking you to be afraid, but definitely be alert.

Last week I attended a memorial for a young man that had committed suicide. No one can figure out any early warning signs. There were no clues. Satan is the father of lies and preys on those who isolate themselves and believe him when he whispers lies into their ears. It was heart wrenching to watch his mother and the rest of his family sobbing. Just for the sake of a little truth, suicide creates more problems, it doesn't solve them. There are so many video games out there where you can just go back and become alive again, start the game over again, but when it says game over in real life, the game really is over. Please make sure your kids know that. One of my kids is an introvert and spends a lot of time alone. This is my conversation with my son after this incident:

Me: Tony, you cannot die before me.

Tony: Mom, we've talked about this before. With everything that's already happened to me, it's highly possible that I will die before you.

Me: Not anymore, it is not right for a son to die before his mother. You can't die before me, ok?

Tony: Alright, I'll try, but you need to understand that if I'm doing something stupid, like driving too fast and wreck, I didn't do it on purpose, but I was having fun, ok?

Me: Ok. (Then I start weeping) Tony, you know the Lord, right?

Tony: (answering without a moment's hesitation) Of course I do Mom, that's why I'm not afraid of dying.

You and I both know this conversation is not realistic, no one can choose when they will die, and even some that attempt to commit suicide survive. But it told me what I needed to know:

1. My son is not suicidal.

2. He knows where he's going.

But keep in contact with your kids even if you think they are too old for a pep talk. NO ONE is EVER too old.

Challenge: Listen to your kids. Pray for your kids. Talk to your kids. Be your kid's cheerleader!

Prayer: God I know that spiritual warfare is real and most of it happens inside our minds. Help us, as parents, to form a relationship with our teens so they can talk to us <u>any</u> time. In Jesus name, Amen

RELATIONSHIPS VERSES BEING RIGHT

Psalm 7:1-5 O LORD my God, In you do I put my trust: save me from all them that persecute me, and deliver me: Lest they tear my soul like a lion, rending it in pieces, while there is none to deliver. O LORD my God, if I have done this; if there be iniquity in my hands; If I have rewarded evil unto him that was at peace with me; (yea, I have delivered him that without cause is my enemy:) Let the enemy persecute my soul, and take it; yea, let him tread down my life upon the earth, and lay my honor in the dust. Selah.

There is a change in the wind. I can feel it. You should never go into business with someone unless there is a signed document. I know this sounds crazy but the closer you are to someone, the more you need boundaries. Why, because the relationship is at stake.

Jason is 21, he is on his own now, and he has a good job. Well pretty good, no insurance and not much room to move up, but it keeps him busy and out of trouble....mostly. I used to be able to boast about how he has never shown me disrespect. Now it is different. There is no more gratitude for being a good mom and no more hugs before he leaves. I wouldn't even think that much of it except for one thing-he didn't respond to my invitation to go out to eat with us or even call. It was Mother's Day. I want to pretend it's not that big of a deal. I don't put much stock in holidays because they are stressful and they put a burden of obligation on people. Abraham Lincoln once said that, "Most people are about as happy as they make up their minds to be." I decided that if I was going to have an expectation for Mother's Day, Christmas, my birthday, or whatever, it would be MY obligation to fulfill it, or at least express it to make it easy for others. I don't want others to feel responsible for my happiness, that's called codependency. If I want a certain meal, or I want to go out to eat, then I go; whoever wants to tag along, they are welcome. Expectations lead to disappointments. I finally figured out that it is my responsibility to drop the expectations or make them happen. BUT we can't control other people, I didn't even know I HAD the expectation that my son should talk to me or at least communicate on some electronic device three words, "Happy Mother's Day." **Psalms 7:8-10 The LORD shall judge the people: judge me, O LORD, according to my righteousness, and according to my integrity that is in me. Oh let the wickedness of the wicked come to an end; but establish the just: for the righteous God tests the minds and hearts. My defense is with God, who saves the upright in heart.**

So what did I do to bring this on? Well that's where the business comes in. His boss leased our land, so it is his job to come out and fix the fences, bring out food for the animals and so on. I volunteered without being asked to be his personal supervisor. I NEVER call him just to say Hello. No, he is not being responsible, and yes, his dad has fixed the fence numerous times...when it is not his job. So you might say, "You have every right to badger and goad and nag him into doing what he should be doing automatically." At what price? Our relationship? That is too high of a price for me to pay. It is not my job to "fix" my son. That bears repeating, "It is NOT my job to fix my son." I raised him and he knows right from wrong. Now the choices are his to make, not mine. It is an inside job, a matter of the heart and only God can fix that. **Psalms 7:14-16 Behold, he brought forth iniquity, and has conceived mischief, and brought forth falsehood. He made a pit, and dug it, and has fallen into the ditch which he made. His mischief shall return upon his own head, and his violent dealing shall come down upon his own pate.** My job is to trust God....lest I fall into the same pit, trying to "play" God.

Psalms 7:17 I will praise the LORD according to his righteousness: and will sing praise to the name of the LORD most high. Sometimes relationships are more important than being right. I should probably read that one over a few more times too. Of course, there are exceptions, including physical and mental abuse. In such a case as that, mental and physical welfare are more important!

Challenge: Trust that God is big enough to change the hearts of our children and make them and mold them into the young men and women that he has called them to be.

Prayer: Lord, please help me to trust you instead of trying to do your job. Please give us the wisdom to love as you have loved us, even "while we were yet sinners". **(Romans 5:8)** In Jesus name. Amen

DAY 8

GUILT SLINGER

Psalm 8:1 O LORD our Lord, how excellent is your name in all the earth! who have set your glory above the heavens. If we truly believe that statement then why do we continue to work out our own problems? Saying it is one thing, doing it is another. If you are going to talk the talk, then you need to walk the walk. **Psalms 8:2 Out of the mouth of babes and infants have you ordained strength because of your enemies, that you might still the enemy and the avenger.** More like out of the mouths of your own children, (no longer babes) two of mine that said, "Just stay out of it Mom." But after the Mother's Day incident, that obviously bothered me more than I realized, I just couldn't keep my mouth shut. Jason's boss had made an agreement with D. Jason was supposed to do his boss's part. He failed to do his part and pulled the, "Yeah, I know, I'll get to it....

Me to D: "This is all your fault, you agreed to this and didn't get anything signed." (Yes, I realize it wasn't all his fault, I am responsible for my own actions!)

D: Remains silent. (Wisely)

Me: It is killing what little relationship we had left.

Raise your hand if you have ever been a guilt slinger! I could've handled that a little differently....like praying about it, surrendering my emotions to God, forgiving D and Jason, find my strength and joy in the Lord instead of in someone else's behavior, considered WHO God is and recognized that HE can handle my emotions, Jason's attitude and everything else. After all he is GOD!

Psalms 8:3-9 When I consider your heavens, the work of your fingers, the moon and the stars, which you have ordained; What is man, that you are mindful of him? and the son of man, that you visit him? For you have made him a little lower than the angels, and have crowned him with glory and honor. You made him to have dominion over the works of your hands; you have put all things under his feet: All sheep and oxen, yea, and the beasts of the field; The fowl of the air, and the fish of the sea, and whatsoever passes through the paths of the seas. O LORD our Lord, how excellent is your name in all the earth!

God is God, he created the heavens and the earth. It is a small thing for him to comfort me, give me the strength to forgive, heal me and be my help in times of trouble. He is Jehovah Jireh, my provider. He is all knowing, He is my Shepherd, He is my Peace.

Me: "I wish you would just take over and do all the things yourself, then we wouldn't have to confront him."

D: "Then he would never learn."

He was right of course, I was once again loving <u>myself</u> more then I loved my son. The ultimate goal was the comfort zone....for me.

Yes, I hugged my husband and apologized and through tears I said, "I just miss him."

Challenge: Find a website or book that list the names of God and their meaning. When we understand WHO God is it is easier to put our trust in him. Oh and sometimes your kids will give you some good advice, don't ignore them.

Prayer: Father you gave me this mother's love for my son, you planted him deep in my heart. I couldn't hate him even if I tried. I just want to hug him and protect him and love him and yes, change him. Forgive me Father for, one more time, trying to do your job. Thank-you for protecting my son, teaching him and watching over him. You are my peace, please bring me to acceptance and peace in this matter and once again give me wisdom in loving your child. Give me patience Lord, I know this is a lifelong journey, not a quick fix. Your timing, your way, your will.

In Jesus name, Amen

DAY 9

BAGGAGE

Psalms 9:15 The heathen are sunk down in the pit that they made: in the net which they hid is their own foot taken.

It was just a question.... one question, but it was the wrong question. I have a rule at my house; no alcohol. Many people have this rule, but my rule is often broken. And sometimes they think enough time has passed that I will get used to it. I'm not used to it. I will never be used to it. It's not fun, it's not funny, and it has NEVER done anything good for me. We can put aside the fact that the partakers might be underage. If they don't do it here they will do it elsewhere. We can put aside the fact that I have stated there will be no alcohol in this house. Most of the time, I'm ignored and they sneak it in after I go to bed anyway. Yes, they are disrespecting me, but they don't see it that way, even my own husband doesn't see it that way. So no wonder he addressed the question a little differently than I did.

So what was the question? "Do you mind if the guys buy some beer and bring it out?" It hit me out of left field, doesn't he know better than to ask a question like that? I was dumbfounded so I said, "Here talk to your dad"...before I blew. But "Dad" handled it differently than I had even considered! "What kind do you want, I have some down at the shop, you can drink that." Now I wasn't just dumbfounded I was mad. WHAT?!!! Not that I care if he has a few beers down at the shop, but it was a totally lack of consideration of my feelings. I ask him, "Do I not have any say of what goes on in my own house?" He said, "It's not in your house; it's down at the shop." It was like trash was falling from the sky, and landing on me. I was trying to dodge it, but I couldn't turn off my memory. The trash was turning into hail stones now. The memories.... The words out of my mouth, "You have obviously not spent much time with an alcoholic, have you?" He didn't respond. What could he say? By now I was carrying around about 30 pounds of baggage on my back. My drunk uncle stepping on my toes while he was teaching me how to dance at a wedding dance. Another wedding dance where my dad broke a bottle on the bar and threatened to kill someone. The waiting for the next shoe to drop, constantly. Carrying out buckets of vomit trying to help my dad recuperate from another binge. The fights, the yelling, ... walking into a hospital and seeing my dad tied to a bed having hallucinations so frightening he was screaming, at first he didn't even recognize me. Hearing about the man who died in the car accident; Dad said he wasn't driving, but he was found in the driver's seat. Letters from the state hospital to his little 10 year old girl and the poem, "if I'd known then what I know now, instead of having one I would have had ten." He lost it, he lost it all. His family, his job, his home, his health, his dignity, his strength, his life.

And more recently, I said to D, "You know your family can sit down and have a drink and appreciate it and very seldom go overboard. Mine can't. If I open the door to that I will have people passed out in the bathroom, talking trash talk and not having any idea that they are in my house and stabbing me in the heart. Please, I don't want that.

I will NEVER think someone acting stupid because they are drunk is funny. I will NEVER believe the excuse of being drunk." I was able to calmly confess my fears to him and I think he understood. I will always be praying that my kids do NOT turn into alcoholics. It's in their blood-the odds are against them....but for the grace of God. **1 John 4:18 There is no fear in love; but perfect love casteth out fear: because fear hath torment. He that feareth is not made perfect in love. Psalms 9:20 Put them in fear, O LORD: that the nations may know themselves to be but men. Selah. Psalms 138:7-8 Though I walk in the midst of trouble, thou wilt revive me: thou shalt stretch forth thine hand against the wrath of mine enemies, and thy right hand shall save me. The LORD will perfect that which concerneth me: thy mercy, O LORD, endureth for ever: forsake not the works of thine own hands.**

Challenge: Trust God with the future of your children. Give your past baggage to God and ask for healing.

Prayer: God please guard them and don't let them destroy the lives of others and drag innocent people down into the pit with them. But in the end, God is God. **Psalms 9:1-4 I will praise thee, O LORD, with my whole heart; I will shew forth all thy marvellous works. I will be glad and rejoice in thee: I will sing praise to thy name, O thou most High. When mine enemies are turned back, they shall fall and perish at thy presence. For thou hast maintained my right and my cause; thou satest in the throne judging right.** Father, my enemy is Satan, I know you can protect my kids, I know you will send your angels to guard them. I've seen it and I trust you. Thank-you.

DAY 10
THE GIFT OF LIFE

Psalms 10:3-5 For the wicked boasteth of his heart's desire, and blesseth the covetous, whom the LORD abhorreth. The wicked, through the pride of his countenance, will not seek after God: God is not in all his thoughts. His ways are always grievous; thy judgments are far above out of his sight: as for all his enemies, he puffeth at them.

As a parent many times we get caught in the middle of desperately trying to keep our children happy. Let me put in this disclaimer; it is not our job to keep our children happy. It started out as a used motorcycle for a birthday gift. D got caught up in the moment, perhaps the reminiscing of his own childhood. Jason talked him into a brand new motorcycle and brought it home with payments. We all have our moments of weakness. Unfortunately D and I were not on the same page. He was working full time and I was home with the crazy "let me grow up now" mess alone. Maybe we should have shared more, prayed more, informed more.... Making payments is not something Jason was used to or even capable of. I struggled to catch D up, telling the future like a fortune teller on one side and griping him out on the other. **Psalms 10:6-7 He hath said in his heart, I shall not be moved: for I shall never be in adversity. His**

mouth is full of cursing and deceit and fraud: under his tongue is mischief and vanity. These are harsh words from the Psalmist but somewhat true. I felt like I could see God's refiner's fire coming. By allowing Jason to talk him into the "gift" D had helped him believe the lie from Satan that he could do and have anything he wanted.... without retribution. He had a few mishaps, and yes, wrecks, but nothing more than a few scrapes. In the midst we prayed for Jason's safety. That was just automatic. When it happened we were more than 15 hours away. When we first received the call I thought Jason was just making a big deal out of nothing, another scape or two..... then the woman on the phone mentioned Care Flight. WHAT? If it's just a broken arm why are they calling Care Flight? As we began our trip home we called in the siblings to stand in until we got there. Praise God for large families! **Psalms <u>10:12 Arise, O LORD; O God, lift up thine hand: forget not the humble.</u>**

I did not feel humble. Even as I type this there are tears in my eyes, because His mercies they fail not! I had to fight my thoughts not to blame D. I had to wrestle with the enemy to not go to the "worst case scenario". But God.....humbled me. **Psalms 10:17-18 LORD, thou hast heard the desire of the humble: thou wilt prepare their heart, thou wilt cause thine ear to hear: To judge the fatherless and the oppressed, that the man of the earth may no more oppress.** Praise God for his hand on Jason that day and his hand on my mouth. I heard Jason speak over the phone, hearing his voice said two things, he was alive, and his brain was still intact. It is possible to still be alive but dead! We praised God. Jason was up and walking within 3 days. He left the hospital with titanium steel in his leg and his arm. There is always something to praise God for. God's grace, God's protection,

God's forgiveness and God's never ending love and life itself is a gift, there are no guarantees.

Challenge: Allow God to humble you....surrender early on rather than trying to hold onto control that was never really yours to begin with. Don't state the obvious! Praise God for life because where there is life there is hope.

Prayer: Thank-you Father for the gift of life. Thank-you for keeping our children safe more times than I even know about. Thank-you that even when I make the wrong choices you are greater. **Psalms 10:1 Why standest thou afar off, O LORD? why hidest thou thyself in times of trouble?** O LORD, you are not hiding, sometimes I just choose to trust my emotions over your truth. **Hebrews 13:5 Let your conversation be without covetousness; and be content with such things as ye have: for he hath said, I will never leave thee, nor forsake thee.** I have a tendency to trust what I see with my eyes instead of believing you are working on our behalf in the unseen. Build my faith Lord, help me to trust you with my children, believe you are listening to my prayers and know that you love my children thousands of times more than I do, and you know what's best for them. Amen

PRAYER IS POWERFUL, WORRY IS WORTHLESS

Psalms 11:7 For the righteous LORD loveth righteousness; his countenance doth behold the upright.

Hebrews 12:5-6 And ye have forgotten the exhortation which speaketh unto you as unto children, My son, despise not thou the chastening of the Lord, nor faint when thou art rebuked of him: For whom the Lord loveth he chasteneth, and scourgeth every son whom he receiveth.

I went for a walk early today. Yes, I wanted to beat the heat, but I also wanted to escape reality. I got a text; "Mom, will you cut my hair?" "I'm not there!" I replied, "I'm on my walk". He got his dad to do it and I wept over a lost opportunity. At the same time I was grateful that I didn't have to be so close to my pain. I didn't want to cry in front of him. He would not have understood my emotions nor appreciated his tough mom acting like a baby. He did not ask me to go with him. He asked his dad. Again, I was grateful. Where were they headed to? Court. I know that many of you reading this have experienced the same thing and possibly for far more serious crimes.

I can't even imagine your pain nor do I pretend to understand the burden you bear. But we have some similarities.

We go over it again and again asking ourselves the same questions, "What could I have done differently?" "What can I do now, without making it worse?" And then the prayers; "God I trust you to work miracles here, may your will be done. May your will be done. May your will be done." Then we wonder, "Is it his will that my child suffer? Was it his will that others suffer because of my child? Surely not. Then we asked, "What exactly is your will Lord?" And then of course Satan steps in with his take on the subject.

As they drove past me they slowed down and stopped, even though I knew they were already running late. Their purpose; to give him a hug and a kiss, so I could touch him one last time, possibly for months. **Job 38:36 Who hath put wisdom in the inward parts? or who hath given understanding to the heart?** Although we train up our children to the best of our ability, many of us relying heavily on God's grace, mercy and wisdom, it is God who puts wisdom into the hearts of the people. Job's children were not just put in jail they were killed along with most of his livelihood taken from him. Job starts complaining (and who wouldn't?!!) And the Lord speaks back starting in Job 38 all the way to the end of 41 reminding Job that God is God and Job is not. And we are not either. I have not heard yet the "verdict" but regardless of what happens God is still God. I can choose to trust him with my son and find peace or not trust him and make myself sick with worry. Prayer is powerful, worry is worthless.

Truth: **Psalms 11:1 In the LORD put I my trust: how say ye to my soul, Flee as a bird to your mountain?**

Challenge: Read Job 38 to 41 just to remind yourself of who God is.

Love your sons and daughters but do not enable them.

Proverbs 26:4 Answer not a fool according to his folly, lest thou also be like unto him.

Psalms 12:6 The words of the LORD are pure words: as silver tried in a furnace of earth, purified seven times.

Prayer: Father please put wisdom in the hearts of our sons and daughters, give them understanding and fill them with truth. Please give them the grace to act on that knowledge, to change, to grow and fulfil your purpose of glorifying you here on earth. In Jesus Name, Amen

DAY 12
PRIDE

What exactly is pride? People say we should take "pride" in our work. Our parents say, "I'm proud of you!" after we've won a game or an award. But for me pride is more of a hindrance then anything, because any time I get prideful I start comparing. From my own experience this is what I know:

1. Pride will always drop me like a rock saying, "You're not good enough."
2. Or pride will make me think I am better than someone else.
3. Proverbs 1:2 When pride cometh, then cometh shame: but with the lowly is wisdom. I would rather have wisdom.
4. It is ALWAYS better when the Lord lifts me up rather than I do it myself. He knows how long I can handle it before I start judging and comparing myself to others.
5. God has a way of lovingly bringing me back to humility and reminding me that He is God and I am not.

This time, however, it felt more like a slap in the face.

There are two groups of friends, those that judge you and try to fix you and those that appreciate you and accept you as you are. I had to stop and ask myself, "What kind of a friend am I"? In all honesty I'm a fixer. But a few years ago I turned over a new leaf. God gave me the message to Love, and "Love is the greatest of these." **1 Corinthians 13:13 And now abideth faith, hope, charity, these three; but the greatest of these is charity.** Still, I have a long ways to go and it takes practice. And it takes opportunities to put myself in someone else's place and see things from their perspective. I know God is on my side. I know that I need to be humbled because I have a problem with judging, pride and comparing, none of which has anything to do with love. **2 Corinthians 10:12 For we dare not make ourselves of the number, or compare ourselves with some that commend themselves: but they measuring themselves by themselves, and comparing themselves among themselves, <u>are not wise.</u>** Mrs. C was the perfect mom. I've never heard her raise her voice. I compared myself to her often. Isn't that always the way it happens? I once heard someone say, "Stop comparing your gooey chocolate insides with their shiny M&M outsides." They had a point and this has stuck with me. Yes, we should support each other, pray for each other and love each other, but not expect their path that God has chosen for them be the same as God has chosen for us. And by the way, it took me a while to find my path.

Psalms 12:1-4 Help, LORD; for the godly man ceaseth; for the faithful fail from among the children of men. They speak vanity every one with his neighbour: with flattering lips and with a double heart do they speak. The LORD shall cut off all flattering lips, and the tongue that speaketh proud things: Who have said, With our tongue will we prevail; our lips are our own: who is lord over us?

My pride: I honestly believed I was doing the right thing. I clung to the idea that I was right and maybe I was, but just because I was doing the right thing doesn't mean everyone else was falling in line. I've finally figured out that there is more than one way to climb a mountain and in spite of that fact that I thought I knew the best way, some choose to ignore my path and take the hard way. Do you want to go up the mountain and see God or do you want to go around the mountain 40 times. I left out a key factor when choosing a path for my kids: They had choices too. I remember the "ah ha moment"…. or I should say moments when I recognized was no longer in control. I kept grasping for it but it seemed to be just out of my reach. My children should have gotten it by now. I specifically and purposefully raised them different than I was raised. They knew the truth, they had DAILY bread but they turned from it over and over again and even doubted the very existence of God. The bottom line is I did it better than most people, especially better than fill in the blank. Hear that pride! OUCH! "Pride cometh before a fall." At least I was home, present, available….but that wasn't enough to keep them from evil. There is no quicker way to be humbled then to find out your son is in jail. There is no easier way to run to God than to find out that you are totally and completely inadequate in stopping the wheels from turning. There is no easier way to learn to give your children over to God then to discover that you are completely and utterly powerless. There is no better place to be when you are totally helpless, needy, and broken than in the presence of God. **Psalms 12:6-7 The words of the LORD are pure words: as silver tried in a furnace of earth, purified seven times. Thou shalt keep them, O LORD, thou shalt preserve them from this generation for ever.**

Proverbs 11:2 When pride cometh, then cometh shame: but with the lowly [humility] is wisdom.

Proverbs 16:18 Pride goeth before destruction, and an haughty spirit before a fall.

Romans 12:3 For I say, through the grace given unto me, to every man that is among you, not to think of himself more highly than he ought to think; but to think soberly, according as God hath dealt to every man the measure of faith.

Challenge: **Micah 6:8 He hath shewed thee, O man, what is good; and what doth the LORD require of thee, but to do justly, and to love mercy, and to walk humbly with thy God?**

James 4:10 Humble yourselves in the sight of the Lord, and he shall lift you up.

Be humble, Love God, Love others and believe that HE IS NOT finished yet.

Prayer: Father thank-you for humility. Please help us to love others unconditionally and to recognize when we fall into the trap of judging others. Give us the grace to accept others where they are at and fill us with your love so we have plenty to give away. According to your will, your riches and glory. Amen.

DAY 13

COMFORT ZONE ADDICT

Psalms 13:2-4 How long shall I take counsel in my soul, having sorrow in my heart daily? how long shall mine enemy be exalted over me? Consider and hear me, O LORD my God: lighten mine eyes, lest I sleep the sleep of death; Lest mine enemy say, I have prevailed against him; and those that trouble me rejoice when I am moved.

Many of us have children that return to the nest temporarily, but it's becoming a habit with Jason. I get so frustrated because I allow him to steal my peace at least three times a week. He comes in after we've gone to bed usually. I woke up this morning and thought I heard a sneeze. My stomach immediately tightens up. You see Jason has this habit of waiting until the very last minute to ask for something and expects us to just jump up and supply him with whatever he ask. What does he ask for? Money, gas, another key, because he lost his. We are learning to say no, but we haven't yet been able to do it often enough or without second guessing ourselves. He keeps catching us off our guard. Naturally, when he's here we can't relax. Like the alcoholic syndrome when I was a child, I'm waiting for the next shoe to drop. Only this time I have a little more control, I CAN say no. So you are thinking, well then what's the problem? The problem is balance. God calls us to, "love thy neighbor as thyself." So we ask ourselves, "How much do we love ourselves"? It's been almost a year, but I remember the conversation vividly. Jason was in jail, and I was contemplating how to get him out. I had already bailed him out of jail 2 or 3 times. I'm praying asking God what to do, and I hear him rebuke me;

"You love yourself more than you love Jason."

"What?"

"It is not Jason you want to help, it is your own comfort."

Ouch! I knew God was telling me a hard truth. I was willing to enable Jason to keep doing what he was doing so I could go home with a clear conscience and feel like a good mommy. I will never forget the day that I walked away from that window. He was saying, "Just sell the car and use that money to get me out." I said, very clearly, "Jason, we are not getting you out this time." I feel like that was one of the hardest things I've ever done. He cried as I walked away.

Now back to the present; Even as I was typing this Jason comes in and says, "If I don't have $280.00 to pay my fine I'm going to jail." I did not offer to pay, I simply said, "I'm sorry." Will D and I be able to stick to our decision and let Jason pay for his own junk? It's VERY important to have a united front. **Galatians 6:7 Be not deceived; God is not mocked: for whatsoever a man soweth, that shall he also reap.** If we enable him God may have to do something more drastic to pull him back to the fold. Have you read Numbers lately? God is not to be trifled with! **Hebrews 10:31 It is a fearful thing to fall into the hands of the living God.** We know what the right thing to do is, but it is a hard thing. My emotional mother's heart wants to rescue, even now, even in my anger and frustrations. But I know better.

Challenge: **Psalms 13:5-6 But I have trusted in thy mercy; my heart shall rejoice in thy salvation. I will sing unto the LORD, because he hath dealt bountifully with me.**

Rejoice in the Lord always, even when you don't understand, even when it hurts, even when everything in you wants to scream.

Prayer: Oh Lord, be our strength. Help us to do what is right in your sight. Give us peace. In Jesus name. **Philippians 4:6-7 Be careful for nothing; but in every thing by prayer and supplication with thanksgiving let your requests be made known unto God. And the peace of God, which passeth all understanding, shall keep your hearts and minds through Christ Jesus.**

DAY 14

JUDGE NOT

Psalms 14:1-3 The fool hath said in his heart, There is no God. They are corrupt, they have done abominable works, there is none that doeth good. The LORD looked down from heaven upon the children of men, to see if there were any that did understand, and seek God. They are all gone aside, they are all together become filthy: there is none that doeth good, no, not one.

Share: Tony: I'm not sure I even believe there is a God any more.

Me: Really? As much as you know about the incredible earth, and as many times as you have looked at the stars with your dad, can you really say that? Only a fool would say there is no God, and you are no fool.

Tony: Well ya, ok your right.

Well that was easy, that was 2 or 3 years ago. Tony is a smart person and given enough time, like his Dad, he can figure things out. He knows who God is, he believes in Jesus Christ as his savior, and he knows where he's going when he dies. Not only that but he knows how to "behave" and can usually get what he needs just by being respectful and well mannered. Because of that he is easy to love. So what's the problem? Like the rest of my children he doesn't go to church. They don't do what a "good Christian" is supposed to do. So I get hung up on things, until I read Psalms 14. NO ONE does what a "good Christian" is supposed to do! That's why we need a Savior!

Paul, one of the best "Christians" ever, had problems. **Romans 7:15-16 For that which I do I allow not: for what I would, that do I not; but what I hate, that do I. If then I do that which I would not, I consent unto the law that it is good.**

Who am I to judge when I constantly have to go back to God for forgiveness of judging others, or anger, or gluttony; and the list goes on. I truly believe that God puts "difficult to love" people in our lives to teach us to love as he loves. Unconditionally, right where they are at. **Romans 5:8 But God commendeth his love toward us, in that, while we were yet sinners, Christ died for us.** He didn't wait until we deserved it, thank God! Accepting others as they are doesn't mean allowing sin to take place right in front of you and not saying anything, but choose your battles. Many of us have preconceived yokes around our necks and believe everyone else should be wearing the same yoke. Are you reading your bible every day? Do you have a daily devotional time? Are you going to church every Sunday? Are you out partying with unbelievers every weekend? **Mark 7:7-9 Howbeit in vain do they worship me, teaching for doctrines the commandments of men. For laying aside the commandment of God, ye hold the tradition of men, as the washing of pots and cups: and many other such like things ye do. And he said unto them, Full well ye reject the commandment of God, that ye may keep your own tradition.** I have to be careful with that judging thing, trying to put Christianity in a neat little box, tied with a bow. I can hear many of you screaming, "But it says to go to church and to refrain from...

and to……" That may be true, but where you are in your walk took you a while to get there. Rome wasn't built in a day, and God is still working in ALL of us. **Philippians 1:6 Being confident of this very thing, that he which hath begun a good work in you will perform it until the day of Jesus Christ:**

Challenge: Resign from being someone's Holy Spirit today. It's not our job.

Prayer: Lord, touch our hearts to love as you have loved us. Use us as vessels to love those who are difficult to love. Give us wisdom to speak the truth in love when we need to, but to choose our battles, because the law kills; but grace brings life. Help us to run to you for wisdom, for council, and to be our refuge when we are confused. In Jesus name, Amen

2 Corinthians 3:6 Who also hath made us able ministers of the new testament; not of the letter, but of the spirit: <u>for the letter killeth, but the spirit giveth life.</u>

Psalms 14:6 Ye have shamed the counsel of the poor, because the LORD is his refuge.

DAY 15

LOVE COVERS A MULTITUDE OF SIN

Psalms 15:1-5 LORD, who shall abide in thy tabernacle? who shall dwell in thy holy hill? He that walketh uprightly, and worketh righteousness, and speaketh the truth in his heart. He that backbiteth not with his tongue, nor doeth evil to his neighbour, nor taketh up a reproach against his neighbour. It is an easy thing to slip into judgement. It says right there that he won't enter in; But none of us will without the blood of Jesus Christ. Then why even try? Why go through all the trouble to tell the truth, to walk uprightly, to …. What difference does it make? Yes, it has already been a frustrating day. Jason can't seem to tell the truth, ever. But this is one of the few times I caught him in it, he turned it around and said if I would get off his back he wouldn't have to lie. Really? I heard him lying to someone last night on the phone and I wasn't on his back then. Then there are times I wonder if he is even capable of telling the truth. Perhaps something inside is handicapped and he doesn't know the difference. Oh he knows. When I caught him he knew. It's nothing to gloat about, it was one time out of a thousand.

"Oh God", I cry out, "How am I supposed to handle this?"

"Love him."

"How do you love a liar and a thief?"

In whose eyes a vile person is contemned; Has my son become a vile person? (Vile: Base; mean; worthless; despicable) No, I don't believe he has stooped that low. **but he honoureth them that fear the LORD. He that sweareth to his own hurt, and changeth not.** Do I fear the Lord? Keep my word even if it hurts me. **He that putteth not out his money to usury, nor taketh reward against the innocent. He that doeth these things shall never be moved.** Never be moved? That seems like a fairy tale, I move with the wind. I hurt, I exalt and I rejoice, I trust, and I doubt all within ten minutes! What kind of person will never be moved? I just read it. 1. Walk upright 2.Work righteousness 3. Speak truth in your heart. 4. Don't gossip or talk evil behind someone's back, do anything evil to them, disgrace or shame or be rude or haughty, (arrogant) toward them. GUILTY! Recently I heard a sermon about forgiveness. At the end of the sermon the Pastor made us repeat after him. "I will not talk about this anymore to anyone." No wonder I've been moved. At first I made the excuse that it is good to talk about it, just so you don't kill the said thorn in your side. Now I see that it is "moving" me all over the place. It's time to pray more than I talk.

Psalms 1:1-3 Blessed is the man that walketh not in the counsel of the ungodly, nor standeth in the way of sinners, nor sitteth in the seat of the scornful. But his delight is in the law of the LORD; and in his law doth he meditate day and night. And he shall be like a tree planted by the rivers of water, that bringeth forth his fruit in his season; his leaf also shall not wither; and whatsoever he doeth shall prosper.

Challenge: Speak life.

Prayer: Oh Father, put a guard over my mouth and help me to speak things that are edifying and useful, honoring you, glorifying you and edifying those that hear. By your grace, Amen

Ephesians 4:29 Let no corrupt communication proceed out of your mouth, but that which is good to the use of edifying, that it may minister grace unto the hearers.

TRUST IN THE LORD

Psalms 16:1 Preserve me, O God: for in thee do I put my trust.

I asked myself, "Do you put your trust in the Lord?" How many times a day have I said, "Never the less, THY will be done, not mine." I believe that no matter how badly I've messed up, missed the boat, or just totally blew it, God is capable of cleaning up the mess. But, yes there is always a "but" in there; when other people are involved there is the free will factor and the Satan factor to contend with, not to mention their own walk with the Lord and them NOT putting their trust in God but in other things.

Psalms 16:4 Their sorrows shall be multiplied that hasten after another god: ... at times even I go after other things before I run to God- food, friends, books, my own wisdom. We are all on a journey, and we will not arrive at our destination until we die; but what if the false gods are money, drugs and alcohol? This is a whole new realm of power that takes on another dimension. It's almost like witchcraft. Such is the case with Jason. Yes, the same one I pegged as a preacher when he was young. I often find myself questioning "what if?" Followed by, "would've, could've, should've". A person can drive them self crazy with that question, so it is imperative that I stay in today. I need to move forward changing the things I can and not looking back at the things I can't change. Satan tries to push me back there, knowing it is a waste of time, not to mention depressing. Would've, could've and should've-ing on ourselves is never productive, and it ALWAYS leads us to losing our faith, hope and joy.

Somewhere along the way Jason crossed over the line. **Ephesians 6:2-3 Honour thy father and mother; (which is the first commandment with promise;) That it may be well with thee, and thou mayest live long on the earth.** We recently found hot checks that were written...out of our account. The worst part about that is that I was not surprised. I could see it coming. But I thought it would be someone else's check book! Jason has shown respect to us in that he has never threatened me, or tried to hit me or even cussed me out. We've argued, but he's always shown some respect. Even when I suspected he was taking cash out of my purse or change out of our change jar and lying to me, he didn't threaten me. For that I was grateful because I've heard stories of other wayward children.

Psalms 16:10 For thou wilt not leave my soul in hell; ... We have to believe that God can handle Jason and all his problems. **Psalm 139:8 If I ascend up into heaven, thou *art* there: if I make my bed in hell, behold, thou *art* there. Romans 8:38-39 For I am persuaded, that neither death, nor life, nor angels, nor principalities, nor powers, nor things present, nor things to come, Nor height, nor depth, nor any other creature, shall be able to separate us from the love of God, which is in Christ Jesus our Lord.**

We also have to trust that God will take care of our property and us. **Psalms 16:5-9 The LORD is the portion of mine inheritance and** of my cup: thou maintainest my lot. The lines are fallen unto me in pleasant places; yea, I have a goodly heritage. I will bless the LORD, who hath given me counsel: my reins also instruct me in the night seasons. I have set the LORD always before me: because he is at my right hand, I shall not be moved. Therefore my heart is glad, and my glory rejoiceth: <u>my flesh also shall rest in hope</u>.** I also have to remember that stuff is just stuff, the real treasures are those we are laying up in heaven. Even so, God has shown us that he will even guard our "stuff"! **Psalms 16:11 Thou wilt shew me the path of life: in thy presence is fulness of joy; at thy right hand there are pleasures for evermore.** Don't get me wrong. We still have our moments of worry. We still struggle to, first of all, figure out the Lord's will-then do it; but when we do, we have peace and even joy in the midst of chaos.

Challenge: **Proverbs 3:5-6 Trust in the LORD with all thine heart; and lean not unto thine own understanding. In all thy ways acknowledge him, and he shall direct thy paths.**

Prayer; Lord help us to make the right decisions concerning our son, take the right actions that will lead him back to you, not to make us comfortable. Help us to make the hard choices to bring him to repentance, not enable him to continue down into the pit he has already dug. Thank-you for watching over him and keeping him safe in spite of the choices he makes. Thank-you for watching over us and our home, reminding us that YOU are our portion. In Jesus name, Amen.

DAY 17

HOPE

Psalms 17:1-3 Hear the right, O LORD, attend unto my cry, give ear unto my prayer, that goeth not out of feigned lips. Let my sentence come forth from thy presence; let thine eyes behold the things that are equal. Thou hast proved mine heart; thou hast visited me in the night; thou hast tried me, and shalt find nothing; I am purposed that my mouth shall not transgress. Oh, if I should be judged by how I make others feel, I would be lost indeed. I would like to confess to you that I am the type of person who speaks the truth in love, but that would be a lie. I have a tendency to call it like it is. Be up front, wear my feelings on my sleeve and be totally honest regardless of how it makes the other person feel. That is all good and well, unless you are ripping someone apart. **Galatians 6:1 Brethren, if a man be overtaken in a fault, ye which are spiritual, restore such an one in the spirit of meekness; considering thyself, lest thou also be tempted. Galatians 6:7 Be not deceived; God is not mocked: for whatsoever a man soweth, that shall he also reap.** Yes, you guessed it. This honest way of handling things came back around and hit me squarely in the face. We were at a board meeting, something I tried to get out of. We were talking about ways to improve our little group when I mentioned a few changes I had made that I thought were helping. The leader of the meeting said and I quote verbatim, "Yes, and I HATE that! In fact it DISGUST ME! Those last two words came out like a hiss. I was of course dumbfounded and it left me speechless with my mind totally blank. Thank God! Because I know if there had been anything in my mind I would have let it all hang out. I surprised myself by speaking very calmly as I picked up my things and stood; "I think that I should leave now so that I will not say something I will regret later." And I walked out. It was only later that it occurred to me that I had talked to Jason that same way. "We no longer trust you, don't you get it, you are untrustworthy." Was it the truth? YES. In fact this verse describes his actions perfectly! **Jeremiah 9:8 Their tongue is as an arrow shot out; it speaketh deceit: one speaketh peaceably to his neighbour with his mouth, but in heart he layeth his wait.** But **"I am purposed *that* my mouth shall not transgress."** Is that possible? **James 3:2 For in many things we offend all. If any man offend not in word, <u>the same is a perfect man</u>, and able also to bridle the whole body.** <u>What if we are to be judged by the way we make others feel?</u> OUCH! And if we are, what exactly should Jason feel after I have spoken to him? My friend came up with that answer without even thinking about it. <u>Hope.</u>

1 Peter 3:8-13 Finally, be ye all of one mind, having compassion one of another, love as brethren, be pitiful, be courteous: <u>Not rendering evil for evil, or railing for railing: but contrariwise blessing; knowing that ye are thereunto called,</u> that ye should inherit a blessing. For he that will love life, and see good days, let him refrain his tongue from evil, and his lips that they speak no guile: Let him eschew evil, and do good; let him seek peace, and ensue it. For the eyes of the Lord are over the righteous, and his ears are open unto their prayers: but the face of the Lord is

against them that do evil. And who is he that will harm you, if ye be followers of that which is good?

70 times 7. Jason is in jail. No we did not have the guts to put him there ourselves, he did it on his own. I will not rescue him but tomorrow I will visit him and love him.

Challenge: Practice the art of forgiving, loving and planting hope in the hearts of the hopeless.

Prayer: Dear Heavenly Father, Please give me the words to speak and my son the ears to hear as I speak life through the power of your Holy Spirit to fill him with hope and love. Satan's favorite ploy is to steal our hope. Guard our mouths Father so we don't become Satan's advocate! In Jesus name, Amen

DAY 18

STEP OUT OF THE WAY

Psalms 18:2-3 And he said, I will love thee, O LORD, my strength. The LORD is my rock, and my fortress, and my deliverer; my God, my strength, in whom I will trust; my buckler, and the horn of my salvation, and my high tower. I will call upon the LORD, who is worthy to be praised: so shall I be saved from mine enemies.

Sometimes I look up in the clouds and I try to make images out of things; I know weird, right? But I don't know anyone who hasn't done it at one time or another. This day, as I was staring at the clouds, I saw a very muscular strong man picking up a set of weights. As I watched the clouds I could see the shape changing. The strong man became limp and a bigger man over him was kneeling down holding him in his arms. The last image was the big man on one knee like he was going to pick him up in his arms and carry him off somewhere. Later when I was looking in my Bible for a whole different verse I found this one. **Psalms 18:32 It is God that girdeth me with strength, and maketh my way perfect.** It had Jason's name written beside it. This was a life verse I had chosen for him. When I saw the cloud change that day I felt like God was speaking to me saying, "I will take his strength away, but don't worry, I will be his strength. **Psalms 18:4-6 The sorrows of death compassed me, and the floods of ungodly**

men made me afraid. The sorrows of hell compassed me about: the snares of death prevented me. In my distress I called upon the LORD, and cried unto my God: he heard my voice out of his temple, and my cry came before him, even into his ears. We, my husband and I, are very much aware that worry and anxiety can bring us to death's door much faster than normal. It will definitely steal your energy and joy if you don't stay close to God. Still many times, even if you are close to God, you can feel the battle raging. So we cry unto the Lord, someone who has felt the battle of the flesh and pours out his grace and love to us. **Hebrews 4:15-16 For we have not an high priest which cannot be touched with the feeling of our infirmities; but was in all points tempted like as we are, yet without sin. Let us therefore come boldly unto the throne of grace, that we may obtain mercy, and find grace to help in time of need.**

Psalms 18:17-18 He delivered me from my strong enemy, and from them which hated me: for they were too strong for me. They prevented me in the day of my calamity: <u>but the LORD was my stay</u>. Before I start picking out who my enemy is, namely the one that is causing me the most stress, remember that we "wrestle not against flesh and blood." **Ephesians 6:12 For we wrestle not against flesh and blood, but against principalities, against powers, against the rulers of the darkness of this world, against spiritual wickedness in high places.** But it is difficult to fight an enemy you can't see, an enemy that can disguise himself, or an enemy that is cunning and secretive when you have a human being right in front of you. Not only that but he is in jail, so he is a captive audience. Still I could hear God saying, "Step out of the way." "But he needs me Lord." "I will take care of him, you are hurting him." Ugh! That was a punch in the gut, but I knew He was right. This was not the first time Jason had been in jail. I had rescued him several times, however, this time I was ready to hear the truth. I had actually been a part of removing his power to make choices and accept the consequences on his own. I gave him someone to blame so he didn't have to look at himself.

Psalms 18:25-33 **With the merciful thou wilt shew thyself merciful; with an upright man thou wilt shew thyself upright; With the pure thou wilt shew thyself pure; and with the froward thou wilt shew thyself froward. For thou wilt save the afflicted people; but wilt bring down high looks. For thou wilt light my candle: the LORD my God will enlighten my darkness. For <u>by thee</u> I have run through a troop; and <u>by my God</u> have I leaped over a wall. As for God, his way is perfect: the word of the LORD is tried: <u>he is a buckler to all those that trust in him.</u> For who is God save the LORD? or who is a rock save our God? <u>It is God that girdeth me with strength, and maketh my way perfect.</u> He maketh my feet like hinds' feet, and setteth me upon my high places. Psalms 18:39 For thou hast <u>girded me with strength unto the battle</u>: thou hast subdued under me those that rose up against me. Psalms 18:46-49 The LORD liveth; and blessed be my rock; and let the God of my salvation be exalted. It is God that avengeth me, and subdueth the people under me. He delivereth me from mine enemies: yea, thou liftest me up above those that rise up against me: thou hast delivered me from the violent man. Therefore will I give thanks unto thee, O LORD, among the heathen, and sing praises unto thy name.**

Challenge: Step out of God's way and learn to speak the truth with love through His grace and mercy towards you.

Prayer: Father please help me to be merciful, upright and pure and not froward with high looks (prideful). Help me to trust you because

I want you to be my buckler (protector, defender, shield). Fill me with the strength of your Spirit so that I can battle the enemy with YOUR power, knowledge and wisdom. Please don't let me be my own worst enemy with my wicked imaginations. Help me to trust in you to be the God of my salvation. Help me to be merciful, upright and pure and believe that you are able bring good out of evil and change all of our hearts. In Jesus name.

DAY 19

HAVE FAITH

Psalms 19:1-3 The heavens declare the glory of God; and the firmament sheweth his handywork. Day unto day uttereth speech, and night unto night sheweth knowledge. There is no speech nor language, where their voice is not heard. How can you look up into the skies and say, "there is not a God"? The millions of stars, the constant patterns and movements cannot have just happened. Any amount of time we spend in nature shows off God's handiwork, his greatest being <u>us</u>! And yet they doubt. The young people question. Is it because we haven't taught them properly. Maybe we didn't go deep enough. Maybe we just expected them to follow in our footsteps and believe what we said because, well, just because! "But where is the proof?" they ask. "How do you know that's real?" Because of 5000 answered prayers, that's how. Because his word speaks to my heart that's why. "I'm just not sure he's real anymore." **Psalms 19:7-11 The law of the LORD is perfect, converting the soul: the testimony of the LORD is sure, making wise the simple. The statutes of the LORD are right, rejoicing the heart: the commandment of the LORD is pure, enlightening the eyes. The fear of the LORD is clean, enduring for ever: the judgments of the LORD are true and righteous altogether. More to be desired are they than gold, yea,**

than much fine gold: sweeter also than honey and the honeycomb. Moreover by them is thy servant warned: and in keeping of them there is great reward. Have you read through the laws lately, they have even caused me to doubt, mainly because I don't understand the purpose of most of them. In my opinion they could've left at least half of them out. But I'm not a scholar, and **Isaiah 55:8-9 For my thoughts are not your thoughts, neither are your ways my ways, saith the LORD. For as the heavens are higher than the earth, so are my ways higher than your ways, and my thoughts than your thoughts.** If I had waited until I understood it all, I would never have believed, that's why it's a faith walk. We taught them about faith, but for some reason, that I don't understand, these young people, our children, who breathed, ate, slept, walked and talked the Word are now questioning it or just simply ignoring it. Did we come on too strong, did we do something wrong. Would a different strategy, or tactic have kept them in church? Kept them from alcohol, drugs and spiritual lethargy? Kept them believing in and living in Jesus? Have they come to the conclusion that they don't need Him? If they can't understand it, it isn't necessary? Why can't they just walk in the light as he is in the light? **1 John 1:5-7 This then is the message which we have heard of him, and declare unto you, that God is light, and in him is no darkness at all. If we say that we have fellowship with him, and walk in darkness, we lie, and do not the truth: But if we walk in the light, as he is in the light, we have fellowship one with another, and the blood of Jesus Christ his Son cleanseth us from all sin.** Your word went forth into their ears, your truth is planted in their hearts. It will not "return unto you void"! **Isaiah 55:10-13 For as the rain cometh down, and the snow from heaven, and returneth not thither, but watereth the earth, and maketh it bring forth and bud, that it may give seed to the sower, and bread to the eater:**

So shall my word be that goeth forth out of my mouth: it shall not return unto me void, but it shall accomplish that which <u>I please</u>, and <u>it shall prosper in the thing whereto I sent it</u>.

Isaiah 40:31 But they that wait upon the LORD shall renew their strength; they shall mount up with wings as eagles; they shall run, and not be weary; and they shall walk, and not faint.

Philippians 1:6 Being confident of this very thing, that he which hath begun a good work in you will perform it until the day of Jesus Christ:

Challenge: Be Patient, Trust God, Keep Loving, Keep praying

Prayer: Father, Teach me to be patient as you continue to do a good work in my children. Help me to wait patiently, keeping my eyes on you not the lack of evidence. I want to believe in your power and love for my children, your children, because I know you love them so much more than I ever could! Help me to walk in faith knowing you will not give them a stone for bread or a snake for fish. Please Father, bring them back to their roots, your word, your truth, your Son. **Matthew 7:9-11 Or what man is there of you, whom if his son ask bread, will he give him a stone? Or if he ask a fish, will he give him a serpent? If ye then, being evil, know how to give good gifts unto your children, how much more shall your Father which is in heaven give good things to them that ask him?** In Jesus name I am asking now.

DAY 20
ALL HAVE SINNED

Psalms 20:1-3 The LORD hear thee in the day of trouble; the name of the God of Jacob defend thee; Send thee help from the sanctuary, and strengthen thee out of Zion; Remember all thy offerings, and accept thy burnt sacrifice; Selah. Psalms 20:7-8 Some trust in chariots, and some in horses: but we will remember the name of the LORD our God. King David had to deal with an assault coming from his own son. It is not unheard of. Even in the midst of his son trying to destroy him David cried out for mercy for his son. There are times that your enemies are within. Who gave Tony his first drink of alcohol? His brother! Who gave Jason his first pot? A trusted friend, and the boy's mother knew about it. Bottom line, we cannot put our trust in our own precautions or so called trustworthy friends. No matter how hard we try the little foxes find a way in and eventually become big problems. So once we've discovered that our control is a façade we go to God. It's important to understand that God never waists suffering. We will always learn something from it. What did I learn? I'm not in charge, God is. **Psalms 20:4-5 Grant thee according to <u>thine own heart</u>, and fulfil all <u>thy</u> counsel. We will rejoice in thy salvation, and in the name of our God we will set up our banners: <u>the LORD</u> fulfil all thy petitions.** What mother in her right mind would pray that her child be caught, found out, and tossed in jail? Most of us are ignorantly soft hearted, but not God. He knows what our children need when they need it. He knows how much they can handle. He knows the right dose of wisdom to pour out at the right time. **20:8 They are brought down and fallen: but we are risen, and stand upright. Save, LORD: let the king hear us when we call.** What made them fall? They trusted in the wrong things, horses and chariots, or in this case, drugs, alcohol...but let's not judge to harshly. How often have we put our trust in the wrong things....or wrong people including ourselves? Because of our pride we think we can do this....as long as we do it right. **Proverbs 3:5-6 Trust in the LORD with all thine heart; and lean not unto thine own understanding. In all thy ways acknowledge him, and he shall direct thy paths.** We were never supposed to be directing our own path or the paths. **Proverbs 16:18 Pride goeth before destruction, and an haughty spirit before a fall.** How often do we try everything else before we pray? Let's face it, most of what we know we learned because of our failures or mistakes. But praise God, **Lamentations 3:21-23 This I recall to my mind, therefore have I hope. It is of the LORD'S mercies that we are not consumed, because his compassions fail not. They are new every morning: great is thy faithfulness.**

Challenge: Step out of the hurricane for a minute, take a deep breath and pray.

Lamentations 3:24-27 The LORD is my portion, saith my soul; therefore will I hope in him. The LORD is good unto them that wait for him, to the soul that seeketh him. It is good that a man should both hope and quietly wait for the salvation of the LORD. It is good for a man that he bear the yoke in his youth.

Prayer: Heavenly Father so many times we have turned to other vices to try to "fix" things. Please remind us to turn to you first. Teach us to trust you. Build our faith so we can know that you have given angels charge over our children and you will be faithful in completing the work that was started in them. Even if it wasn't started Father it's not too late for you. **"The LORD hear thee in the day of trouble"** and **"send thee help from the sactuary"** and strengthen us and our children. Direct all of our paths and remind us to run to you first, not last.

DAY 21

LETTING GO

Psalms 21:1-2 The king shall joy in thy strength, O LORD; and in thy salvation how greatly shall he rejoice! Thou hast given him his heart's desire, and hast not withholden the request of his lips. Selah. Just a few more weeks until the family reunion, and he's coming. It will be his first time to come to our house since the theft. We were devastated, heart sick and ready to vomit when we discovered it. He actually paid a high price for his dishonor towards his parents. We suspected it, knew in our hearts but couldn't prove it. But this was different, it wasn't just money. How long ago, who knew? We never checked. Were we gullible, just plain stupid? How could this have gone so wrong, so very wrong? **Psalms 21:11-12 For they intended evil against thee: they imagined a mischievous device, which they are not able to perform. Therefore shalt thou make them turn their back, when thou shalt make ready thine arrows upon thy strings against the face of them.**

I was holding the old fashioned phone in my hand as I looked at him through the glass. D was standing behind me waiting for his turn. I was afraid he wouldn't have the heart to set the boundary so I did.

"You cannot come back to the house because of what you have done, you understand that, right?"

"I don't really have anywhere else to go."

"It doesn't matter, you can't come home."

It was easier to say this time. I had had a revelation (surely wisdom from God). In trying to help we were actually causing things to get worse. Each new action was a little bit bigger, a little bit worse. By this time I had been in Celebrate Recovery for several months. I had learned that the best thing I could do for Jason was to hand him completely over to God and be totally honest. It was freeing to realize it wasn't my job to fix him anymore. Of course it never really was to begin with.

He was in jail and headed to prison this time. Because of the devastation he had left in his wake, this time, I had come to the conclusion that prison would be the best place for him. **Psalms 21:8-12 Thine hand shall find out all thine enemies: thy right hand shall find out those that hate thee. Thou shalt make them as a fiery oven in the time of thine anger: the LORD shall swallow them up in his wrath, and the fire shall devour them. Their fruit shalt thou destroy from the earth, and their seed from among the children of men.** I was ready to "Let Go and Let God". When I got to this point I was empty, strung out and detached. The book says to detach with love but I felt nothing, like a void in my heart. Then in the next minute it would change, I was crying over all that could've been, crying over the future of my beloved boy. But he was not a boy any more, he was a man and would be tried as a man. We were put in a position that we actually had evidence of another crime in our home. Talk about a split personality. I told God I would not call them but if they called me I would tell them the truth, the whole truth and nothing but the truth. Not only did the detectives call, they came to our house. D and I sat together at the table and told the whole truth. We may as well have handed them the key to the cell. Ironically for the first time I felt calm, and in the middle of God's will. In the end he did not go to prison but was put on parole, only God could've orchestrated that. Not only did he not go to prison he got his old job back along with a place to live! What God? I can't spoil him but you can? Of course he can, God can do anything he wants to do.

Psalms 21:13 Be thou exalted, LORD, in thine own strength: so will we sing and praise thy power. Romans 9:14-18 What shall we say then? Is there unrighteousness with God? God forbid. For he saith to Moses, I will have mercy on whom I will have mercy, and I will have compassion on whom I will have compassion. So then it is not of him that willeth, nor of him that runneth, but of God that sheweth mercy. For the scripture saith unto Pharaoh, Even for this same purpose have I raised thee up, that I might shew my power in thee, and that my name might be declared throughout all the earth. Therefore hath he mercy on whom he will have mercy, and whom he will he hardeneth.

Challenge: Who do you need to let go of and turn over to God today? Do it....over and over if necessary because we Moms have a tendency to pick it right back up again.

Prayer: Father, Thank-you for the mercy you've shown to my son.... your son. Please Lord continue to watch over him, direct him away from trouble, pull him out of the mirery clay, and away from the sin that "doth so easily beset him". Thank you that you love him much more than I ever could and you have not left him, and you will not forsake him. Please keep him in the palm of your hand and draw him ever closer to your truth. In Jesus name.

DAY 22

FAITH 101

Psalms 22:1-My God, my God, why hast thou forsaken me? why art thou so far from helping me, and from the words of my roaring? O my God, I cry in the daytime, but thou hearest not; and in the night season, and am not silent. But thou art holy, O thou that inhabitest the praises of Israel. Our fathers trusted in thee: they trusted, and thou didst deliver them.

I feel like I've been kicked in the teeth with reality. I hate this feeling of defeat. I hate feeling totally useless, helpless, and vulnerable, like my very soul has been cut to the quick. What grace? I remember saying, after reading the book,[Don't Let Your Kids Kill You by Charles Ruben] how difficult it would be to have two. How impossible it would be to find joy or peace when the only two kids you had were constantly lying and into drugs and all kinds of other things. I feel defeated, I want to yell out, "you won Satan, you win, just kill us all and let us go home". I know, pretty dramatic, right? In this state I am not useful for anything accept destroying someone else's faith with my doomsday, unbelief, raw emotions. What? Did I not pray enough, pray too much, be too proud, put them on a pedestal, set them up for a fall, expect too much, give too much, be too much, not be enough? **Psalms**

22:6-8 But I am a worm, and no man; a reproach of men, and despised of the people. All they that see me laugh me to scorn: they shoot out the lip, they shake the head, saying, He trusted on the LORD that he would deliver him: let him deliver him, seeing he delighted in him. And on this day you time the beautiful picture of the perfect family arriving in a Christmas card! Is that how all the other people felt when I sent my pictures out? Were they just waiting for the shoe to drop? Did they think we were pious, proud, gloating? Did they not see that I was trying to build my kids up because I knew the fire was coming? I wanted them to have positive loving memories to fall back on when the hard times came. Somewhere deep in my heart I knew they would come. **Psalms 22:9-11 But thou art he that took me out of the womb: thou didst make me hope when I was upon my mother's breasts. I was cast upon thee from the womb: thou art my God from my mother's belly. Be not far from me; for trouble is near; for there is none to help.** Lord Tony was your child that YOU planned. He was our surprise, our gift of grace straight from you. Hope, where is this hope? Oh God, I am weak, come and pick me up. **Psalms 22:14-16 I am poured out like water, and all my bones are out of joint: my heart is like wax; it is melted in the midst of my bowels. My strength is dried up like a potsherd; and my tongue cleaveth to my jaws; and thou hast brought me into the dust of death. For dogs have compassed me: the assembly of the wicked have inclosed me: they pierced my hands and my feet.**

Tony was getting ready to graduate. We were so excited, he was at the top of his class. He was offered a top notch job. They were reconsidering their offer. Tony was never very good at lying. "What is the holdup," I asked? They found trace drugs in the drug test. Why did you tell me? To dump the trash? No, he was tired of lying to me? And now you are headed back there, with that same person that pulled you in, or you pulled in, at this point who knows? Smart? They decided they should sample it. They called themselves smart because they chose a good reliable resource. It was pure.

Psalms 22:19 But be not thou far from me, O LORD: O my strength, haste thee to help me.

Even smart people can do stupid things. Part of me wishes you would have kept your mouth shut. Part of me is glad you trusted me enough to tell me. I feel like part of me has died. I know the author though, because you called yourself smart for doing something so stupid. Do you know that Satan is the father of lies? Do you know that when you are deceived you don't know you are deceived? Satan is always calling the good bad and the bad good. Karma really? But I will pray for you. Why? Because that's ALL I can do. **Psalms 22:20-21 Deliver my soul from the sword; my darling from the power of the dog. Save me from the lion's mouth: for thou hast heard me from the horns of the unicorns.** He got the job, they do regular long term drug testing which means he can't continue taking it. Yes, God is still on the throne and even in the midst of free will he can make things happen.

Challenge: Have faith in Jesus and His power even when you can't see it happening.

Prayer: God be patient with us, we are strong in the Spirit but weak in the flesh, weak in faith, weak in living for you. We expect comfort, an easy road of joy and happiness - in many ways you have provided that, building our faith, drawing us to you. Yet at the first sign of trouble we want to quit, give up and go home. Build our strength Father, we can do nothing without you. In Jesus name, by your grace, in your strength.

DAY 23

LISTEN

Psalms 23:1-3 The LORD is my shepherd; I shall not want. He maketh me to lie down in green pastures: he leadeth me beside the still waters. He restoreth my soul: he leadeth me in the paths of righteousness for his name's sake. As the Lord shepherds us we are to shepherd our children but when does that stop? Hopefully as our children grow up and they transform into a friendship relationship rather than a parent/child relationship. If we are still telling our 25 year old what to do then there is something wrong with the picture. If we are offering advice or making a suggestion that's different, but there is a fine line. I am in a group therapy program called Celebrate Recovery. I have an ongoing problem of continuing to "mother" my children. If you want to get a little more vicious you can call it what it is, "playing God". I am better, so much so that I often say, "I don't want to hear it." It's so much easier to NOT get mad, try to fix it or play God when you don't know. There's another reason I don't want to hear it especially if it is about alcohol consumption; it's a trigger as you have seen on day Day 9.

Psalms 23:4 Yea, though I walk through the valley of the shadow of death, I will fear no evil: for thou art with me; thy rod and thy staff they comfort me. When my kids were younger I had been overwhelmed with lying. I told all my kids, you can tell me anything, just tell the truth, but what if one of my kids wants to talk and I don't want to hear it. What if someone wants to talk to you about alcohol consumption? We are really close, in fact we are good friends, "I was really having a problem a few weeks ago, Mom, but I couldn't come and talk to you about it because <u>you wouldn't listen</u>." It hit me hard that in my quest to protect myself from worrying I was shutting out my own children when they needed a sounding board. The absence of worrying, I have discovered, isn't the art of sticking your head in the ground, <u>it's trusting that God is bigger.</u> Not just bigger than any problem that I have but bigger than any problem my kids have. **Psalms 23:5 Thou preparest a table before me in the presence of mine enemies: thou anointest my head with oil; my cup runneth over.** Satan is our greatest enemy, but everywhere he is God is there too. God is everywhere, omnipresent. Satan is not omnipresent. God sees all, he knows all, but sometimes we need someone with skin on.

God can and will equip me and prepare me to move forward to do his bidding, triggers, hangups and all. He calls imperfect people to do his perfect will. I realize I need to be available and trust God to cover my blind spots and my vulnerability as well as those old memories that creep in. He knows them all, and he knows me too well to allow me to selfishly protect myself when I'm needed. I know the end of the story. When I get to heaven I would rather hear God say "Well done my good and faithful servant" rather than, "Where the heck were you?" **Psalms 23:6 Surely goodness and mercy shall follow me all the days of my life: and I will dwell in the house of the LORD for ever.**

Challenge: Believe that God can use you in spite of you or your hang ups and ask him to show you when you need to slow down and listen.

Prayer: Lord please help me to be available when you call me to listen to someone else. Give me the wisdom I need to comfort them and guide them to the cross and into your grace. **2 Peter 1:5-9 And beside this, giving all diligence, add to your faith virtue; and to virtue knowledge; And to knowledge temperance; and to temperance patience; and to patience godliness; And to godliness brotherly kindness; and to brotherly kindness charity. For if these things be in you, and abound, they make you that ye shall neither be barren nor unfruitful in the knowledge of our Lord Jesus Christ. But he that lacketh these things is blind, and cannot see afar off, and hath forgotten that he was purged from his old sins.** Fill me with these things so that I can be fruitful for your sake, glorifying you, praising you and being "meet for the master's use". 2 Timothy 2:21. In Jesus name Amen.

THE GRACE OF GOD

Psalms 24:1-5 The earth is the LORD'S, and the fulness thereof; the world, and they that dwell therein. For he hath founded it upon the seas, and established it upon the floods. Who shall ascend into the hill of the LORD? or who shall stand in his holy place? He that hath clean hands, and a pure heart; who hath not lifted up his soul unto vanity, nor sworn deceitfully. He shall receive the blessing from the LORD, and righteousness from the God of his salvation. Praise God that we live in the "Grace Age". After the death of Jesus Christ we were grafted in because he didn't just die for the Jewish people he died for the Gentiles. If we believe that Jesus Christ died for us we are covered in His blood and we will be with Him in heaven. Again I say, "Praise God", because how many of us can raise their hand and say I have clean hands and a pure heart and I have never..... Lord Jesus, Thank-you for your sacrifice!

Psalms 24:6 This is the generation of them that seek him, that seek thy face, O Jacob. Selah.

Sadly this is NOT the generation that seek him. Many of our children that were tried and true and ready to work for the Lord got distracted. Did we accidently help in this mess? Possible, but in the end each person is responsible for their own belief and their own actions. Somewhere, along the way, they may have met people who were not real, who were not genuine and they decided that this Christian thing wasn't all it was cracked up to be. They took their eyes off of Jesus and Satan jumped in. How can you prevent that? I still question that often. What did I do wrong? I could see one walking away but all five walking away from the church. Again, they saw discrepancies, they didn't take into consideration that these were human beings. People only arrive where they are at because of the grace of God NOT by their own merit. With me being their mom and counting how many times I've had to apologize to them for reacting the wrong way, they should have known. Maybe it was just an excuse. I can drive myself mad with this so I turn to the Lord. The answer I keep hearing is, "I'm not done yet." **Psalms 24:7-8 Lift up your heads, O ye gates; and be ye lift up, ye everlasting doors; and the King of glory shall come in. Who is this King of glory? The LORD strong and mighty, the LORD mighty in battle.** This is the Lord's battle not mine. I will once again turn it over to Him. And you know what? He can handle it! Not in my timetable but his. I'm also exaggerating, my kids still call me and say, "Can you please pray about this?". That doesn't mean they are where they are supposed to be but it also doesn't mean that they have lost their faith completely. Even if they had, it's too late. The Holy Spirit has sealed them. **Ephesians 1:13 In whom ye also trusted, after that ye heard the word of truth, the gospel of your salvation: in whom also after that ye believed, ye were sealed with that holy Spirit of promise,** and he's not finished. **Philippians 1:6 Being confident of this very thing, that he which hath begun a good work in you will perform it until the day of Jesus Christ:**

Challenge: Learn from your mistakes but don't live in the past. Focus on Jesus and his unlimited power, remember he loves our children a thousand times more than we ever could. Believe that God is greater and he is able.

Prayer: Father, we pray not just for our children but for future generations. Please guide them back to the cross, the truth and your grace. Surround them with your love and fill them with your wisdom. Hold them close, direct their paths draw them with your loving kindness. In Jesus name, Amen

Philippians 4:5-7 Let your moderation be known unto all men. The Lord is at hand. Be careful for nothing; but in every thing by prayer and supplication with thanksgiving let your requests be made known unto God. And the peace of God, which passeth all understanding, shall keep your hearts and minds through Christ Jesus.

DAY 25

SEX

Psalms 25:2-3 O my God, I trust in thee: let me not be ashamed, let not mine enemies triumph over me. Yea, let none that wait on thee be ashamed: let them be ashamed which transgress without cause. Remember not the sins of my youth, nor my transgressions: according to thy mercy remember thou me for thy goodness' sake, O LORD. When we are dealing with teenagers it's important to listen, not just to what they are saying but what they are not saying. How much of a struggle do adolescent boys go through to try to stay pure? Why would God put such incredible longings and curiosity in the midst of their already out of control adolescent minds. It baffles me! They eventually just gave up and took the easy way out and more or less got on the train with everyone else. There is something to be said for youth pastors. Yes, we all have a choice and hormones are going wild in both girls and boys but in hindsight I wish I could have better prepared them. **Psalms 25:4-6 Shew me thy ways, O LORD; teach me thy paths. Lead me in thy truth, and teach me: for thou art the God of my salvation; on thee do I wait all the day. Remember, O LORD, thy tender mercies and thy lovingkindnesses; for they have been ever of old.**

We have a tendency to talk about the elephant in the room, but not this elephant. In a society where there are internet and phones galore, it is so easy to come by, no one gets away untouched, some against their will. My advice, no one gets a phone, a tablet, a computer or anything else until they are 16 and driving but even then they are naïve about protecting themselves. We are opening up our kids to 1000 predators and 1000 willing participants just waiting for them to make the wrong move. Yes, you will be the meanest parents on the planet. And be careful with those overnight stays with that wonderful family down the street. Yes, you will be thought of as a paranoid, crazy parent but it's worth it. I was naïve. I thought we were safe. I thought my kids were mature enough to handle it. As a Christian parent trying to raise Christian kids this was a huge hindsight is 20/20. Apparently it is possible. What did I miss? Even now I struggle with the acceptance of "In today's world that's just the way it is Mom." **Psalms 25:7-9 Remember not the sins of my youth, nor my transgressions: according to thy mercy remember thou me for thy goodness' sake, O LORD. Good and upright is the LORD: therefore will he teach sinners in the way. The meek will he guide in judgment: and the meek will he teach his way**. In the end I have no choice but to love them and pray for them. Yes, I can talk to them and tell them the truth, but they already know the truth. **Psalms 25:11-12 For thy name's sake, O LORD, pardon mine iniquity; for it is great. What man is he that feareth the LORD? him shall he teach in the way that he shall choose.**

Yes, Lord, I hand them over to you, their conscience, their future happiness, their successes and their failures. I understand that they can't come on board the righteous rail train just because they know the truth. I should know this because of my own history. I cannot cast the first stone.

Psalms 25:20-21 O keep my soul, and deliver me: let me not be ashamed; for I put my trust in thee. Let integrity and uprightness preserve me; for I wait on thee.

Challenge: Let God do his job and you do yours. Pray, teach truth, trust God and pray some more.

Prayer: I pray Lord that you will give me the wisdom and strength to turn this over to you. Please protect our children Lord Jesus. I am not their Holy Spirit, I am not you and do not need to try to do your job. You have called me to love. Help me to love and give me patience to wait on you. By your grace, through your power, in Jesus name.

DAY 26
HELP

Psalms 26:1-6 Judge me, O LORD; for I have walked in mine integrity: I have trusted also in the LORD; therefore I shall not slide. Examine me, O LORD, and prove me; try my reins and my heart. For thy lovingkindness is before mine eyes: and I have walked in thy truth. I have not sat with vain persons, neither will I go in with dissemblers. I have hated the congregation of evil doers; and will not sit with the wicked. I will wash mine hands in innocency: so will I compass thine altar, O LORD: No one was innocent, but D and I were going to try to focus on loving kindness. We received the phone call at about 1:00 AM. One of those phone calls you don't want to get. "Dad, I flipped my car, I need your help." We asked all the questions; Are you ok? Where is it? It was in the middle of the field. They got the wild idea to go spin "kitties" on someone's private property. Better than the middle of the road I guess.

D said, "Call your brother and asked him to help you flip it back over."

Tony: "I will, but will you please come?"

He was pretty shook up, he needed a parent. This didn't happen very often anymore. Warning: Once they get their driver's license your influence is pretty much done. Pour it in while you still can!

Now we were both awake so we both went. Find something to be thankful for, namely he's alive! **Psalms 26:7 That I may publish with the voice of thanksgiving, and tell of all thy wondrous works.** Stay calm. Don't tell them what they already know, namely, "You screwed up!"

When we rounded the corner we see lights and many cars. Jason meets us, driving a car we don't recognize and pulls even with us to talk. The first thing out of his mouth is, "I feel like I've been violated!" Apparently, not knowing what to expect the police pulled him over. Once Jason saw that the police were there he intended to just keep on going right on past. I'm not judging him, he'd already been in enough trouble with the police so he was right to avoid trouble. They stopped him, pulled them all out of the car, searched them, questioned them and finding out that Jason was the brother sent them on their way. **Psalms 26:9-10 Gather not my soul with sinners, nor my life with bloody men: In whose hands is mischief, and their right hand is full of bribes.** These were kids, mischief? Yes. Sinners? Yes, but aren't we all. I am constantly reminding myself of the scripture; **1 Corinthians 13:13 And now abideth faith, hope, charity, these three; but the greatest of these is charity.** Love is the greatest, not being right, not speaking truth (that they already know) not berating them in shame....Tony already felt bad enough. We walked up to the officer and he immediately identified us as the parents. He proceeded to tell us that they "may have scared Jason a little bit" almost gleefully, like they had done it on purpose. "But he was VERY polite through the whole thing." Another thing to be grateful for, thank-you Jesus! Side note: Mamas teach your children to be polite, show respect and how to give a firm handshake and open a door for a women. Shyness is not an excuse! Respect can open a lot of doors. **Psalms 26:11 But as for me, I will walk in mine integrity: redeem me, and be merciful unto me.** God was merciful! The officer said to us, "I'm going to say that "you" called the tow truck instead of me. The place they chose is private property, provided I can find the owner and they don't press charges there will be no charges." Tony also new to be polite to the officer and I think it paid well-that and the grace of God. D took the car home, beat the dents out of it and Tony drove a not so nice looking car.... perhaps teaching him a valuable lesson! In the future he will buy his own car....and take VERY good care of it.

Challenge: Stay calm. Think before you speak. Speak life. Thank God for his grace over your children.

Prayer: **Psalms 26:12 My foot standeth in an even place: in the congregations will I bless the LORD.** Father please teach our children, young adults, to find the even place, and to join with the congregation in blessing the Lord, thanking the Lord and living for the Lord. Thank-you again and again for your grace and mercy and setting your angels over them, protecting them in their foolishness and helping us love them through it. In Jesus name. **Psalms 91:11 For he shall give his angels charge over thee, to keep thee in all thy ways.**

DAY 27

GRACE

They were headed to Boy Scouts, Tony was driving, D was in the passenger seat. **Psalms 27:1-3 The LORD is my light and my salvation; whom shall I fear? the LORD is the strength of my life; of whom shall I be afraid? When the wicked, even mine enemies and my foes, came upon me to eat up my flesh, they stumbled and fell. Though an host should encamp against me, my heart shall not fear: though war should rise against me, in this will I be confident.** Tony hadn't been driving very long, in fact he still had a learners permit. Apparently both he and D were very tired. Within a couple of miles after they had made the turn, BOTH were asleep. The car veered off the road to the right and Tony over corrected. He went across oncoming traffic, had there been any, spun around and landed in the ditch. Still right side up. Other than a bruise, a minor cut that needed stiches and a scratch they were fine.

Psalms 27:5-6 For in the time of trouble he shall hide me in his pavilion: in the secret of his tabernacle shall he hide me; he shall set me up upon a rock. And now shall mine head be lifted up above mine enemies round about me: therefore will I offer in his tabernacle sacrifices of joy; I will sing, yea, I will sing praises unto the LORD. Why us? I can name off relatives that did not fare so well. They died at a young age. How does God choose? **Psalms 27:8 When thou saidst, Seek ye my face; my heart said unto thee, Thy face, LORD, will I seek.** Tony was not seeking God's face. Had there been oncoming traffic they could have both been killed. D could've died and Tony would have had to live with that for the rest of his life. Grace! **Psalms 27:9-10 Hide not thy face far from me; put not thy servant away in anger: thou hast been my help; leave me not, neither forsake me, O God of my salvation. When my father and my mother forsake me, then the LORD will take me up.** Just like God continues to love us through our faltering we are to continue to love our children. Did he learn anything? Fast forward.... a few months later. Tony calls me up, in the middle of the day. "Mom, they aren't going to let me drive home, can you come and get me? "They", being the police. Tony started feeling drowsy so 5 miles from home he pulled over to the side of the road and went to sleep. A passerby saw him and knocked on the window and was unable to wake him so he called the police. Finally, Tony woke up, but that was after an ambulance, fire truck and police car were on their way. To say Tony is a heavy sleeper is putting it mildly. **Psalms 27:11-12 Teach me thy way, O LORD, and lead me in a plain path, because of mine enemies. Deliver me not over unto the will of mine enemies: for false witnesses are risen up against me, and such as breathe out cruelty.** When D and I arrived Tony had been checked over by the paramedics and was taking a royal chewing from the police officer. She began to tell me all the things she found in his car, expecting me to be shocked.... This child is the one that tells too much truth so I wasn't shocked. By God's grace there were no drugs and no open containers, just a tired boy inside the car. **Psalms 27:13 I had fainted, unless I had believed to see the goodness of the LORD in the land**

of the living. I approached Tony and hugged him and said, "Thank-you for pulling over, I'm glad you're alive."

I heard a quote recently, "If you are still alive, God is not done." **Psalms 27:14 Wait on the LORD: be of good courage, and he shall strengthen thine heart: wait, I say, on the LORD.**

Challenge: In the midst of your children finding their way to the cross let them see Jesus in you.

Prayer: Thank-you Lord for reminding me that you are still working, still active and still loving my children. Help me to respond with loving kindness as I watch them stumble, looking other places for wisdom instead of coming straight to you. Pour out your grace upon them Lord, hold them close, draw them back to you with your loving kindness.

Jeremiah 31:3 The LORD hath appeared of old unto me, saying, Yea, I have loved thee with an everlasting love: therefore with lovingkindness have I drawn thee. In Jesus name

DAY 28

PRAY WITHOUT CEASING

1 Thessalonians 5:17 Pray without ceasing.

Is Satan attacking my family, or is God trying to get their attention?

Psalms 28:1-3 Unto thee will I cry, O LORD my rock; be not silent to me: lest, if thou be silent to me, I become like them that go down into the pit. Hear the voice of my supplications, when I cry unto thee, when I lift up my hands toward thy holy oracle. Draw me not away with the wicked, and with the workers of iniquity, which speak peace to their neighbours, but mischief is in their hearts.

Satan has struck a blow to my peace this week….at least I think it was Satan. Remember that my children were brought up in the Lord, but none go to church regularly nor are they living the "Christian" lifestyle. Just a few weeks ago it was revealed that I am going to be a grandmother….FINALLY!! Is it one of my married children? No, it is Jason and his girlfriend Andrea. She already has a two year old from another father, so this one will be his little half-brother. In ALL things be thankful. Thank you God that they didn't come to me and say they were getting an abortion. They chose life. Now there is a chance, very slim, but still a chance that this new precious little boy, still in the womb may not be "healthy". These are the things that nightmares are made of. I am pleading with God, but how many others have pleaded and their pleas have not been answered? Look around. What will they do if they find out that it is positive? Oh God, have mercy! I had to actually come around to say thy will be done, but I'm still thinking, please Lord, let MY will be done. What grandmother wouldn't pray that? What is the purpose of this? Please Lord. To build our faith? What is the purpose of any disease, sickness, problem or even death at a young age? To draw people to God, but so many are running from God. Many are picking up guns, taking drugs, alcohol, sex, or whatever it takes to deal with their pain, boredom, or emotions.

Psalms 28:4-6 Give them according to their deeds, and according to the wickedness of their endeavours: give them after the work of their hands; render to them their desert. Because they regard not the works of the LORD, nor the operation of his hands, he shall destroy them, and not build them up. Blessed be the LORD, because he hath heard the voice of my supplications. Please DON'T give them according to their deeds but **Romans 5:20 Moreover the law entered, that the offence might abound. But where sin abounded, grace did much more abound**: Let grace abound in the midst of them Father. Show them your mercy, please.

He said he wouldn't give a snake to our children when they asked for bread but are my children even talking to God.

Psalms 28:6-9 Blessed be the LORD, because he hath heard the voice of my supplications. The LORD is my strength and my shield; my heart trusted in him, and I am helped: therefore my heart greatly rejoiceth; and with my song will I praise him. The LORD is

their strength, and he is the saving strength of his anointed. Save thy people, and bless thine inheritance: feed them also, and lift them up for ever.

Challenge: Can you say with Jesus, "Nevertheless, thy will be done." Practice trusting him even when he says no...or not yet. **Proverbs 3:5-6 Trust in the LORD with all thine heart; and lean not unto thine own understanding. In all thy ways acknowledge him, and he shall direct thy paths.**

Prayer: Father you ARE my strength and you are their strength too, but what if they don't know to ask for it. I will ask for them. Give our children strength Father. Help us to trust you, help us to rejoice. Work miracles. God we need you in a big way, we need you in our hearts and in our minds and in our schools. We need you in our midst, fighting the battles that are raging-lying to our children and dragging them into the pit, or worse, teaching them how to dig their own pit. Please Father, move in a mighty way through this country, through our families, through our children, in our hearts and souls. In Jesus name.

FORGIVENESS

Psalms 29:1-2 Give unto the LORD, O ye mighty, give unto the LORD glory and strength. Give unto the LORD the glory due unto his name; worship the LORD in the beauty of holiness. When it said "give unto the Lord" I never imagined that he meant for me to give my children back to him. **Psalms 29:3-4 The voice of the LORD is upon the waters: the God of glory thundereth: the LORD is upon many waters. The voice of the LORD is powerful; the voice of the LORD is full of majesty.** When He first talked to me about it I was terrified. Would he love them as much as I did? Will he take good care of them? These questions are laughable now but back then I was holding on with an iron fist. God had to show me that he was bigger, he was greater, he knew more and he loved my children a thousand times more than I ever could. **Psalms 29:5-7 The voice of the LORD breaketh the cedars; yea, the LORD breaketh the cedars of Lebanon. He maketh them also to skip like a calf; Lebanon and Sirion like a young unicorn. The voice of the LORD divideth the flames of fire.** This entire Psalm talks about how powerful he is. It was ridiculous that I thought I could do a better job. I still shudder with the picture in my mind as I lay them on the altar like Isaac. And yes, I had to do it over and over again. I have a tendency to pick it back up, or feel like I need to remind God of their needs, but in spite of me, God still moves.

It was Thanksgiving. All of our children were going to be home this time. This was not the case last year. Jason was in jail. It didn't stop us from giving thanks to the Lord but there was a definite sadness in the air. Jason had dove into one illegal activity after another. I still feel like I prolonged that because of my own selfishness of enabling him to believe all would be well no matter what. But that is in the past that I cannot change. This time he was here with our new grandchild. I honestly believed he would look at things differently as a new father and I think he has. He has never asked for forgiveness or offered to make amends but D and I chose to forgive anyway, albeit with caution and boundaries this time. I used to feel guilty because I still suspected and had a distrust but forgiveness and trusting are not the same thing. A friend told me, "You didn't break the trust, he did." I let it go. This was a day of celebration, a new start and a new life with a beautiful healthy baby boy. In the midst of Jason's incarceration I asked him; "What do you want out of life? Where do you see yourself in 10 years?" I expected him to say, "Having my own construction crew. Driving a new car. Winning the lottery...." None of that. "Having my own family." Now he does.

We have a tradition in our family where each person stands up and tells of 2 or 3 things they are thankful for. Tony stood, looked at his dad, looked at Jason, and his voice cracked. He barely got Jason's name. That was all. Everyone knew what he intended to say, "I'm glad he's here." This is a miracle. We all know people who won't even talk to their family. A month before this, shortly after the baby was born, all four siblings drove to our house to meet their new nephew! Again, this was a miracle. They saw our struggle, they felt our pain, yet they chose to come and support their brother and his new family. **Psalms 29:11 The LORD will give strength unto his people; the LORD will bless his people with peace.** Our God is able. Forgive, not forget, not throw caution to the wind. **Matthew 10:16 Behold, I send you forth as sheep in the midst of wolves: be ye therefore wise as serpents, and harmless as doves.**

Challenge: Forgive, **Matthew 6:14 For if ye forgive men their trespasses, your heavenly Father will also forgive you:**

Prayer: Oh God, help my son to be a good example, a good father, keep him from going back into all the lying and junk that he was into. Guard his heart Lord for the sake of his children. Give him the wisdom and strength to make wise choices. Help him to come to you, to listen to your voice. Protect his children and their mom and lead them to the cross, to your guidance, and your strength and your love. Thank-you Father for loving my children...your children. In Jesus name, Amen

DAY 30
PAY ATTENTION

Psalms 30:1-2 I will extol thee, O LORD; for thou hast lifted me up, and hast not made my foes to rejoice over me. O LORD my God, I cried unto thee, and thou hast healed me. Tony broke his arm, not just a little bit but a "lot of bit". It required surgery. He has a full time job so he would be off for quite a while. God intervened and found the perfect place, the perfect doctor and the perfect time for the operation. He had also signed up for disability, another God thing. I said please pay attention because God is trying to get your attention. He didn't. He got bored and did some really stupid things. He got a DWI. In the midst of ranting at God I heard the question in my heart, What are you grateful for? Grateful? I yelled....then it came to me.... oh Lord, thank-you that no one was killed! Thank-you that my son is still alive! I began to be a mom, asking myself, "What can I do to help him?" Then I stopped and said, "wait a minute, this is "not my monkeys, not my circus." Then I had to stop myself again and say, "Yes it is your monkey because you never fully gave THIS "monkey" over to God. Ok, well I need to get that taken care of." After church today I went to the alter and handed Tony over to God. I'm sorry to say it's not a one-time deal. I have to do it over and over again. I keep trying to pick it back up. I need to call him, I need to send scriptures, I need him to get it this time! **Psalms 30:3 O LORD, thou hast brought up my soul from the grave: thou hast kept me alive, that I should not go down to the pit.** God allowed him to go into the pit, overnight, for the first time. For Jason this would've been "old hat" stuff, but for Tony it was new. He normally makes good decisions, considering the consequences, anger and alcohol don't mix. **Proverbs 3:7-8 Be not wise in thine own eyes: fear the LORD, and depart from evil. It shall be health to thy navel, and marrow to thy bones. Psalms 30:5-8 For his anger endureth but a moment; in his favour is life: weeping may endure for a night, but joy cometh in the morning. And in my prosperity I said, I shall never be moved. LORD, by thy favour thou hast made my mountain to stand strong: thou didst hide thy face, and I was troubled. I cried to thee, O LORD; and unto the LORD I made supplication.** He was moved, but God loves him and will provide for him all his needs according to His riches and glory. I have no room to judge Tony. I did a lot of stupid things in my childhood. Thank God for His protection through my stupidity and his.

Challenge: Think twice before judging others harshly. **Matthew 7:1 Judge not, that ye be not judged.**

Prayer: Give my son the grace, Lord Jesus, to cry out to you, to ask for your mercy and grace. Give him the grace to be grateful to you, to call your name, to pray to you. Give him favor in spite of his wavering faith. Draw him with your loving kindness, let him feel your presence, your peace, your love, but especially show him wisdom and knowledge and give him the power to act on it. **Psalms 30:8 I cried to thee, O LORD; and unto the LORD I made supplication. Psalms 30:10-12 Hear, O LORD, and have mercy upon me: LORD, be thou my helper. Thou hast turned for me my mourning into dancing:**

thou hast put off my sackcloth, and girded me with gladness; To the end that my glory may sing praise to thee, and not be silent. O LORD my God, I will give thanks unto thee for ever. Please do this for your child. And Lord if,... no, <u>when</u> he does need help please provide it for him, In Jesus name.

DON'T LOSE FAITH

Psalms 31:1-3 In thee, O LORD, do I put my trust; let me never be ashamed: deliver me in thy righteousness. Bow down thine ear to me; deliver me speedily: be thou my strong rock, for an house of defence to save me. For thou art my rock and my fortress; therefore for thy name's sake lead me, and guide me.

Last week at church one of the pastors officially resigned. He stated family's health for his reason but I sensed that he was simply burnt out. A church can do that to you. I went up and told him thank-you for his service and I mentioned that I remembered him ministering to my boys many years ago. His response-"Yeah, for all the good it did them." I did not take offense. Being a youth Pastor is probably one of the hardest jobs and most disappointing jobs in the church. And being a pastor is not much easier. You get to hear everyone's problems and every down fall and just when you think someone has "arrived" you find out there is a secret sin in their lives. During the teen years there is a lot of learning, falling and growing. Of course that continues until we die but it seems more evident when we are young. And don't forget we have an enemy, taking advantage and wreaking havoc! **Psalms 31:4 Pull me out of the net that they have laid privily for me: for thou art my strength.** That is the key! We alone are not strong, no matter how much we try to be or how much we practice. **Psalms 31:5 Into thine hand I commit my spirit: thou hast redeemed me, O LORD God of truth.** We need to surrender to God's will and we need to teach our kids to surrender. God has begun a good work in my children and I believe he will continue it. For the last three days Satan has rocked my world but I am keeping my eyes on Jesus instead of the waves. My kids are paying attention. God has their attention and he will not give up. He will continue wooing them to him until the day they die. **Psalms 31:7-8 I will be glad and rejoice in thy mercy: for thou hast considered my trouble; thou hast known my soul in adversities; And hast not shut me up into the hand of the enemy: thou hast set my feet in a large room.** God is moving. Once again through all the waves he is showing mercy. He wants to talk to them, to guide them, but first he had to get their attention. **Psalms 31:10-11 For my life is spent with grief, and my years with sighing: my strength faileth because of mine iniquity, and my bones are consumed. I was a reproach among all mine enemies, but especially among my neighbours, and a fear to mine acquaintance: they that did see me without fled from me.**

The bottom line is this; no matter how bad it gets don't give up, don't give in and don't stop praying. Seeds were planted by that pastor many years ago and they are still being planted. I pray that my kids know these are not just random things that happen to them, they are divine appointments. **Psalms 31:24 Be of good courage, and he shall strengthen your heart, all ye that hope in the LORD.**

Challenge: Trust that God is still working and keep praying.

Prayer: Heavenly Father I know that my kids have many more battles to fight before they surrender to you. Even I am still working on complete surrender daily. But I trust in you, Father and I'm grateful that you are not just my God but you are God to my kids too. Their times are in your hand and I know you will deliver them from the enemy. Thank-you for your mercy towards them, help them to call on you. Oh how great is your goodness towards the ones I love. Teach them the fear of the Lord and teach them to trust you. Blessed be the LORD: and thank-you Father for showing your marvelous kindness to my children. You have heard my prayers and answered them but more importantly my kids, no, YOUR kids, are seeing those answers too, by your grace and through your power. Teach them to love you Lord, help them to be faithful. Thank-you Lord for loving my kids more than I do. Amen